Angie,

I hope that you find a smile in each and every day as you must always remember that you are deserving. Welcome to the family.

Crystal Thomas

THE UNFORGIVABLE

*If the Walls Could Talk,
Would You Listen?*

CRYSTAL A. THOMAS

Copyright © 2022 by Crystal A. Thomas.

All rights reserved. No part of this book may be reproduced in any form or by any electronic or mechanical means, including information storage and retrieval systems, without permission in writing from the publisher, except by reviewers, who may quote brief passages in a review.

This publication contains the opinions and ideas of its author. It is intended to provide helpful and informative material on the subjects addressed in the publication. The author and publisher specifically disclaim all responsibility for any liability, loss, or risk, personal or otherwise, which is incurred as a consequence, directly or indirectly, of the use and application of any of the contents of this book.

WRITERS REPUBLIC L.L.C.
515 Summit Ave. Unit R1
Union City, NJ 07087, USA

Website: *www.writersrepublic.com*
Hotline: *1-877-656-6838*
Email: *info@writersrepublic.com*

Ordering Information:
Quantity sales. Special discounts are available on quantity purchases by corporations, associations, and others. For details, contact the publisher at the address above.

Library of Congress Control Number:		2022916650
ISBN-13:	979-8-88536-730-1	[Paperback Edition]
	979-8-88536-731-8	[Hardback Edition]
	979-8-88536-732-5	[Digital Edition]

Rev. date: 09/26/2022

"This book is based on actual events in the life of the author as truthfully as recollection permits. While all persons within are actual individuals, some names and identifying characteristics have been changed to respect their privacy."

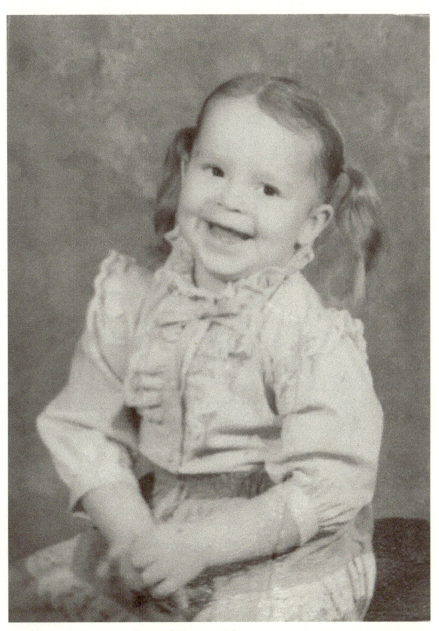

Crystal Burton-Thomas, age 3

Contents

Chapter 1 1
Chapter 2 7
Chapter 3 10
Chapter 4 15
Chapter 5 21
Chapter 6 24
Chapter 7 30
Chapter 8 34
Chapter 9 40
Chapter 10 46
Chapter 11 51
Chapter 12 54
Chapter 13 57
Chapter 14 60
Chapter 15 63
Chapter 16 66
Chapter 17 72
Chapter 18 77
Chapter 19 82
Chapter 20 87
Chapter 21 89

I dedicate my success and gratitude in life to my children, who motivate me to never lose hope and who always give me a reason to keep pushing forward in life. I have no doubt that I wouldn't be here to today without them.

I also dedicate my gratitude to my husband for always giving me the encouragement to keep striving forward, for accepting me for who I am, and for always loving me unconditionally.

Chapter 1

People often reminisce about things in their past that make them smile or happy. Passed down from parents to their children and so on are a bunch of family traditions, memorable times, and bonding moments. But what if most of your memories have been locked away in Pandora's Box because they are too dark or too traumatizing to recall? Would you dare to bring them back, or should you just let them go? But what most people do not realize is that memories are lessons in life whether they are good, bad, or ugly. You either live by them, die by them, or learn from them.

My memories have been locked away in Pandora's Box inside my head for most of my life. It has been a struggle mentally and physically to make the decision to open that box and release those memories that have caused so much trauma in my life. I thought that by keeping them locked away, I was safe. So I didn't have to think about them anymore. Over the years, some of those memories became black holes in my memory that I couldn't recall. But somehow, I have come to learn that they have only robbed me of my emotions, stopped me from feeling loved, and hindered me from exploring my full potential. I've had to learn how to not be a victim but a survivor and advocate to others who understand what I'm struggling with. There are days when I have to close the box and put it away because everything is too overwhelming to take in. There are days when I become so angry and can't continue, days when I literally go right back to that moment, that day in time.

My story began long before I was conceived. My mom was born in the mid-1950s. She came from a family of seven children. Her dad, my grandfather, was a military man, a Korean War veteran. His life ended tragically at the age of thirty-two after he was shot in the head during an altercation with a man after going to his house to pick up his family where my grandmother was visiting with the man's wife in East Prairie, Missouri. At the time, my mom was only nine. He was killed on her birthday. She later spoke about this traumatic event, yet the details she gave were very vague. She wasn't really open about saying too much about it. We could tell that it was a story she did not like talking about; therefore, it was rarely discussed. I'm sure you can imagine the trauma it must have caused her to witness her father getting shot in the head in front of her.

Rita (mom) & Larry (dad) Burton, 1970

My mom and dad got married on May 2, 1970. She was fourteen years old, and my dad was twenty-two. This didn't seem to be anything uncommon in those days as age didn't seem to matter. In their early years of marriage, Mom got pregnant early on, and she gave birth to my oldest brother before she was fifteen. They were living in Tennessee, in the regions of Jackson and Lexington. I only recall Mom speaking about one job that she had when she was with my dad, and that was at the shoe factory. Other than that, I think most of her time was spent raising us kids.

I was born in Lexington, Tennessee. I was the youngest of five children—three girls and two boys. I can't really tell you anything about that part of my life as it is a memory that is just not there. Mom and Dad divorced when I was just a baby, maybe two or three years old. I can't recall any of those memories. I just remember one day he was there and then he was gone. I can't even recall what he looked like. I recall seeing him shortly after they separated when I was around two or three. I was in a room with several adults standing around, and he was standing across the room, trying to get me to come to him. With candy in his hand, he asked me to come get it while I held onto my mom's leg tightly. I remember her saying, "Go ahead." For some reason, I was scared. I knew he was my dad, but I was scared of him. I ran and grabbed the candy from his hand and tried to run back to my mom, but he grabbed me and tried to hug me. I was scared and began to cry, and he let me go so that I could run back into my mom's arms. Little did I know that it would be the last time I would see my dad for many years.

The only memories that I had of my dad are from the stories that Mom told us about him over the years—stories of him being an alcoholic and how she dealt with his physical and mental abuse for years. There was an incident where he held her head down and ran scalding water across her face in the sink. She worked to support us while he continued to drink heavily. One day, he was there, and the next, he was not; it was like he just vanished. Then one day, after a heated argument with my dad, she loaded us in the car, and we left Tennessee to make a home in Missouri. She could no longer tolerate the physical and mental abuse from him.

Being as young as I was when they separated, I immediately forgot everything about life before Missouri. As for Dad, out of sight, out of mind. The only memories of him were spoken stories about him from mom. So how was I to miss a man who seemed like a monster?

Mom's family lived in the Missouri Bootheel, and that was where we moved to—a small town called New Madrid that sat right on the Mississippi River. Not long after we moved to New Madrid, my oldest brother, Rocky, was taken back to our dad. Mom said that Rocky wanted to live with Dad and didn't want to stay with us, so she gave him what he wanted. She said that since he was a teenager and was upset that she was not with our dad anymore, it caused some animosity, and he refused to listen to her.

It all happened one day when Mom was working on a house that we were planning to move into so that we could get out of the run-down trailer park that we were staying in. I was in the living room, playing, when Mom and Rocky suddenly got into an argument. All I remember was the yelling, and then it goes blank after that. Years later, I was told by Mom that, at the time, she was on a ladder, and Rocky walked up where I was standing and hit me in the back between my shoulder blades, knocking me to the floor. I remember their argument somehow, but I cannot remember that he hit me or knocked me down. I was young—that was probably why I could not remember what happened.

It was that day that Mom packed Rocky's things and took him back to Tennessee. She was afraid that my dad would not let her leave, so she stopped at the sheriff's station and told the sheriff that she was leaving my brother there and that he was going back to stay with our dad. The sheriff told Mom that she did not need to worry and that he would take my brother down to Dad's. As we headed back to Missouri without my brother, I didn't know that I would not see him again and that our relationship would soon be forgotten.

My memory of those years is vague and scattered. Mom began going to the bar with her mother and aunt. Not long after that, she met the man who would soon become my stepfather—Wayne. He began buying us toys and coming around all the time. It did not seem like much time passed until she married him. I was very young, maybe four. He was so nice to us. He would take me out for ice cream when the others went to bed. I could stay up late because I was the baby. Nothing really seemed abnormal then.

We were like any other family struggling to make ends meet. He and Mom began to drink quite a bit. I got my first sip of Busch beer from sneaking one of the many cans that I would find sitting on the table. I found the taste disgusting. We would go to parks and have picnics with my Aunt Murl and walk the Big Oak boardwalk. I sat around while they played rummy, and I listened to their laughter as they played; they always swore my brother Joker was cheating. Those was the good memories that stuck.

Then my stepdad began to come home late at night drunk. I could hear them yelling and fighting as he stumbled through the back door that opened into the kitchen. My sisters and I would run to the doorway of our room just to peek out and look, then run back to bed if they got close to our room. I would not say that my childhood at that time was so horrible—just the typical alcoholic in the family that ended the days with arguing while being drunk. But that's normal, right?

We were dirt poor growing up. We collected commodity food, used food stamps, and wore hand-me-downs from garage sales and thrift stores. But what we had always seemed good enough for us. We made do with what we had, and we appreciated what we got. We had what I thought was the normal life. We played outside with the neighbors' kids, rode bikes and big wheels, and played on the tire swing in the front yard. As soon as the streetlight came on, Mom would yell at us to come in and get ready for supper. The girls shared a room together. We would sit up at night talking and giggling, and we spent days playing Shirley and Grandma. I do not know how I ended up always being the grandma, even though I was the youngest.

Mom soon gave birth to my little brother. He was born in a small hospital in Hayti, Missouri. We called him Bub. I was so excited for my little brother to come home. When he came home, I could not stop looking at him. I wanted to hold him and play with him. It was fun having a little brother around. To me, he was perfect. I would later find out that Bub was mentally and physically handicapped due to the choices that the physician made that night when he was delivered. His umbilical cord was wrapped around his neck, and the physician decided to pull him through anyway, causing my brother to be deprived of oxygen for quite some time. Although the doctors kept telling mom that he was just fine, she knew that he was not. He did not learn to walk and talk like most; those things were delayed. The smile on his face when I would pick him up and lug him around was priceless. He was almost as big as me.

The drinking habits of my stepdad and mom continued along with the arguing, but it was different now. It did not seem as intense as before. A few years later, Mom gave birth to my youngest brother, Tony. There were now six of us at home. We had a big family, but it felt like we were all alone. There were no family friends or any other people who came over other than my great-aunts from both sides of the family. They would both watch us while Mom and Wayne were away. I never knew where they went, though. My grandma and grandpa on my mom's side really had nothing to do with us. I barely knew who they were. Mom barely spoke of them. We would see rarely our uncles and aunts, so that was like seeing strangers.

I never really understood why none of our parents' families had anything to do with us. But one thing was for certain—they all seemed to be better off financially than we were. We lived eating the same meal most nights. I watched Mom in the store count out those paper food stamp coupons as she took things out of the cart to pay for our groceries. At the time, I didn't even know what those were. Even though we did not have as much as many other people, we were happy if we had one another. My brothers and sisters were my best friends. They were all I knew and all I had. Little did I know that things would soon change and in the worst way possible.

Chapter 2

I'm not sure what happened to cause the change that was beginning to take place in our lives, but it was not for the better. My stepdad easily became angry for no reason at all. He yelled and cussed like we had never heard before. He soon began to pick on us for the smallest things. One night, as we were sitting around the kitchen table, eating a meal that we all hated, which was beans, he said that we were not allowed to leave the table until they were all eaten. If we did not eat it, he would push the back of the chair closer to the table and demand that we eat them. If we would try to sneak up and not eat, he would jerk his leather belt off his waist in preparation to whoop us. We waited to hear the cling of the belt buckle as he jerked it off his waist, ready to hit the first one of us in his reach. One night, my sister was made to eat them until she threw up. Then she got into trouble for throwing up and had to clean it up. The disgust of seeing brown beans that have been vomited up and the smell have haunted me all my life. I have not eaten or cooked another brown bean meal.

We would spend our summers hanging out at auction buildings or at the baseball field. My stepfather, from time to time, would help out at auctions. My older brother Joker was a great baseball player, and he did very well in school. He won spelling bee competitions and even went to the state spelling bee competition. Wayne, my stepdad, was the coach of the baseball team. My siblings and I spent a lot of time playing at the park on the slides and swings while the baseball games were happening. We had so much fun going to the games. I would sit on the counter in the concession stand and help Mom work the concession stand. Joker was so happy when he played ball. His smile was so big as he grinned with excitement after games. But in Wayne's eyes, he was never good enough. He would compare him to the other boys, most of whom were older than Joker. Wayne was so hypocritical about the games and would criticize the way my brother played. I dreaded seeing the game end because I was afraid of the kind of mood my stepfather would be in. I was not sure if he was going to start yelling at Joker or just say nothing at all. I prayed for the silence.

One night after a baseball game, while we were on our way home, Wayne and Joker began arguing about the game. Wayne was so mad that they lost the game, and he blamed it on my brother and the stupid plays that the other players on the team made. Before I knew it, my stepfather hit Joker in the nose, and blood started to pour down my brother's face. I was frightened, as I had never seen this before. I did not understand what was happening. Mom and Wayne began to argue about him hitting Joker, while we, the kids, went on into the bedroom.

That was the beginning of it all. The hits with the belt were nothing compared to what was ahead. The fighting and arguing began to get even worse. Joker seemed to catch most of it. I would begin to cry as soon as it started, yelling for him to stop. "Don't hit him!" I would say. But Wayne continued as if he didn't even hear me. As Joker got older, he began to fight back, which only made things worse. Wayne had begun to work as a farmer, and I would always dread seeing him come home in fear of what was going to happen when he did. We would try to avoid these situations by going outside and staying until dark or just staying out of his way. Just when we thought we had it figured out on how to avoid him, he ended up injuring his back at work after stepping off a tractor. After that, he was at home all day every day. This was the beginning of our hell on Earth.

Childhood home, the trauma begins here

Chapter 3

The good memories were soon replaced with horrible ones, which I would keep repressed as deep dark secrets for many years. The small town of New Madrid, Missouri, where we lived, would hold secrets that would torment me throughout my life—secrets that made me feel ashamed and embarrassed to talk about, that would tear my family apart and create a wall between us forever.

Wayne had other children from a previous marriage, and we didn't find out about this for several years. We were never told anything about them until one day, an older girl showed up at the house late at night. She was with a friend of hers, and she came in and began talking with Wayne. They laughed and hugged, and I figured they must know each other. She told me that night that she was my sister and that he was her dad. She seemed fun and carefree, something that I wished I could be. She stayed for a few days, and then she was gone. I never knew what really happened. She was just gone. I could tell that Mom didn't like that she was there. There had to be a story behind that, and we would never know the truth because we never went around his other kids or even knew much about them. He did not have much to do with them, nor did he ever talk about them.

I was around four years old when Wayne allowed my stepbrother Little Wayne Jr. to come live with us. It was our first time meeting him, and he was moving in. He was around sixteen or so. I remember him being nice to me, as I was the little sister. I used to be scared to go to the bathroom by myself, so I would beg my sisters to go with me. They would get frustrated and, at times, would ignore me because it seemed to take them away from doing what they were doing. He would always volunteer as they soon got tired of stopping what they were doing to take me to the bathroom. He would take me into the bathroom and turn his head while

I did my business. I just didn't like the feeling of being alone in there. I always had a sense of fear.

One day, we were all watching a movie in the living room when Little Wayne called for me to come to the front bedroom, where he was sitting on the edge of the bed. With the way the beds were set up, I could only see his back as I walked into the room. He asked me to come over to him. I walked around the end of the bed and walked in between the beds to the one he was sitting on. When I looked up at him, I saw that he had his penis out in his hand. He grabbed me by my arm and pulled me over to him.

When I started to pull away, he said, "I won't take you to the bathroom anymore when you're too scared to go by yourself." He then took my head and pushed me down toward his penis. He said, "Put it in your mouth and lick it like you do candy."

He touched his penis to my mouth, and I started to cry because even at four, I knew this wasn't right. Maybe it was from fear of getting caught that he turned me loose when I cried. I ran out of the room. I was confused, scared, and unsure what I should do or say to anyone. So I didn't say anything at all.

A few weeks later, I heard Mom, Wayne, and Little Wayne arguing. It was loud, but they quieted down if my sisters and I were close enough to hear. A little while later, his bags were packed, and we were being told he was going back home. I was not sure what happened, but I was happy that he was gone. Years later, my oldest sister, Allie, told me that he had raped her that day. She said that she told Mom what he did to her, and that was the consequence. No one ever spoke of it again after that.

While Mom tried to work to support us, my siblings and I became the caretakers of our two younger brothers. While Wayne lay around on the couch all day, watching Westerns or ball games, we were forced to take them outside to play from sunup to sundown. The door was locked as we walked out and very rarely were we allowed in—but not without consequences. Summer, winter, fall, and spring . . . it did not matter how hot or cold we were outside with them. We would ride bikes, play house or hide and seek, and do anything that kept us occupied. We made the best of it. We made mud pies and grass salads and used our bikes as cars. If we got thirsty, we drank from the water hose. The only time we were allowed in the house was to go to the bathroom, and then we were yelled at for fanning the door.

I was not sure what happened to make Wayne hate us so much, but it really began to show. Maybe it was the fact that we were not his children. The look in his eyes when he spoke to us was as if he was talking to an enemy that he hated. It was obvious that his boys were treated differently. They were never disciplined for anything. If they did something wrong, we were punished for letting them do it or for making them cry when we didn't want to go back outside.

My stepfather took them to the racetrack and got them ice cream and cheeseburgers every night for dinner while we had to eat whatever was available. Mom cooked supper every night, and our meals usually consisted of white beans, fried potatoes, and cornbread, while Wayne would always get pork chops or pork steaks cooked for him. We rarely got meat, unless it was bologna, but on Sundays, Mom would fry chicken for us. That was our favorite meal. We were not allowed to eat the chicken breasts, as those belonged to Wayne.

After dinner, we had to look at the list on the refrigerator to see whose dish night it was, as we were all assigned nights. After the dishes were done, he would come into the kitchen to inspect it. Everything had to be cleaned and put in order, and if the dishes were not clean, he would throw them all back into the sink and yell, "Do them again!"

While all the kids around us were doing what kids did with their families, we lived very differently. We never really had friends; it was just us. We took care of one another. My middle sister, Cheryl, and I were the closest because we were close in age. Joker and Allie were closer because they were closer in age. We did everything together.

One morning, not long after we awakened, Cheryl came to me and said, "I have something to tell you." We went to our room and sat on the bed. She looked around to see if anyone was coming into the room. I was excited. I thought she had a juicy secret to tell me about Joker or Allie, as we loved picking on them just as much as they loved picking on us. Cheryl took forty dollars out of her pocket and handed it to me. My eyes widened, and I wondered where she had gotten that kind of money from. I asked her where she got it, and she told me that Wayne had given it to her. I was shocked, as we never had money.

I asked her why he gave her the money, and she began to cry. She told me that he had been coming into our room at night and touching her in bad places. I was confused. How could this be happening? Seeing my sister ashamed and embarrassed by this was very upsetting to me. I was supposed to protect her because she and I slept in the same bed. How could I have not known this was happening? I assured her that I was going to tell Mom about what happened because Cheryl was too afraid to tell.

That afternoon, I walked up to Mom while she was in the kitchen, and I handed her the money. She asked me where I got it from, and I told her what Cheryl had told me that morning. She told me that she would take care of it when Wayne got home. We went outside and stayed because we were afraid of what would happen when he got home. Cheryl and I were sitting on top of the deer stand in the backyard when we heard his truck drive up. We sat there as if we were invisible. We strained our ears, trying to hear any yelling or fighting.

As hours passed and darkness approached, we remained in our spot at the top of the deer stand. We heard a car drive up and noticed it was his aunt. We climbed down to see what was happening. We saw him bringing some of his things out to the car. She said to us, "Aww, you're sad to see your daddy leaving, aren't you?" We remained silent and returned to the backyard, hoping that he would be gone soon. Shortly after, we heard her car drive off. We decided it was safe to go inside now, so we called for our siblings and went inside.

As we walked through the front door, we see Wayne and Mom having sex on the couch. I was disgusted and confused. Why was he not leaving? How could she have sex with the man that touched her daughter inappropriately? We ran into our bedroom and stayed there quietly. After a while, I heard Mom in the kitchen.

I walked into the kitchen and asked her, "Why is he not leaving?"

She stated, "Things will be fine. It won't happen again."

I was mad at her and hurt.

That night, Cheryl and I made a pact that we would always be together no matter what. We would never allow each other to be alone around Wayne again, and if one of us was in trouble or needed help, we would do a three-clap warning signal to alert the other that something was wrong. Once again, like before, the incident was never spoke of again. Life went on, and our days were like ground hog day. Nothing changed. It just continued to get a little bit worse.

As time passed, the physical abuse began to worsen between Wayne, Joker, and Allie. He stayed away from Cheryl after that incident. Therefore, he would look for any reason to bring his anger out on Joker—beatings with belts that left welts, punches to the face, choking, pushing, or anything that he could do to inflict pain. I was quietly building anger inside me that would soon become uncontrollable. As the youngest child, I did not get the worst of the beatings at this point. Joker and Allie would get mad at me because they felt like I was being treated better than they were. They would always say that Mom and Wayne liked me better than them because I never got hit like they did.

If only they knew the hurt in my heart every time I had to witness them getting hit with a belt, the feeling of not being able to do anything to help them. It just was not fair. I always wondered if other kids had to go through this at home. Were other parents like this to their kids? Was this normal? I had no idea what life as a child was supposed to be like or how real parenting felt. I was just accustomed to how things were because that was all I knew at this point.

Chapter 4

Fast forward to the early 1990s, about four years later. We moved into our new home. We were so excited. We were finally going to have home that belonged to us. It was somewhere new, and we hoped for a new beginning. It was a new way to try to leave the darkness behind us or only make it easier to contain it in a place that didn't belong to anyone else. The only thing was, darkness wasn't left behind; it followed.

Not long after moving into our new home, Cheryl began her freshman year in high school. She got her first boyfriend, Michael, and he became close with the family. He came to the house daily. My sisters and I would spend our free time in our room, listening to music, dancing, and imagining what life would be like in our future. At times, Mom would turn on the record player when Wayne was gone and the sound of Madonna's "Like a Virgin" or "Papa Don't Preach," "Footloose," or Prince's songs would loudly play as we sang and danced. That would be one of the few times I remember seeing Mom smile.

We were introduced to some people who owned a pig farm in the country on the outside of New Madrid, and Wayne would soon begin helping on the farm. Not long after that started, it somehow became ours to deal with. We never really knew what happened to the people that had it. Wayne just said that they just up and left, which honestly never sat right with me. Michael helped on the farm. The farm became somewhat of an enjoyment as we did not go anywhere else. We had no friends come over, nor did we go places. There was rarely anyone else that ever came over to the house. We had pigs, goats, chickens, and cows. They were fun to play with. But even that got old as we grew older and were not allowed to enjoy life as other kids did.

The farm became a daily routine. As Wayne drove the truck down a gravel road, we had to walk and carry water jugs to water the pigs. When they got out, we had to chase them until we got them back into the pig pen. Getting them back in could take hours. One day, Allie and I were trying to get one of the male boars back into the pen, and Wayne yelled at us, telling us to stand in the middle of the road with a 2 x 4 wood stick and block the boar when he came running in that direction. We were supposed to guide him to go into the pen. An oversized breeding boar weighing almost 600 pounds soon came, and Wayne expected us to stop the boar and corral him into the pen. So as Allie and I stood there, waiting, we saw the boar coming up the road. He was coming full force, and all we could hear were the snorts and clicks of his hooves on the gravel. He looks up at us and then lowers his head, and we could see that he had no intention of stopping or slowing down.

Wayne yelled, "Stop him! You better not let him through there!"

Cheryl and I looked at each other, and when the boar was about a foot from us, we stepped to the side as it was obviously going to be us that was taken down if we continued to stand there. We could see the anger on Wayne's face.

He snatched his hat off his head and threw it to the ground, yelling, "God dammit! I fucking said don't move and don't let him through. Ya'll are fucking worthless!"

I yelled back, "I ain't fixing to stand there and let him knock me down. He ain't scared of that stick, much less me."

Wayne then pushed toward me and pushes me out of the way, causing me to step onto a board that drove a protruding nail in the center of my right foot. I slowly pulled it off the board, and I limped back to the truck so Mom could look at it. She said, "You'll be fine it was just a nail." I couldn't understand why she would let him treat us like this. Why were we treated like we worked for him?

One day, Mom and all of us kids went to go tend to the farm. It was about five miles from home. I believe Wayne was at an animal auction that night. I didn't mind the days we went when it was just us. Mom would make it fun. We played around, and she let us drive the truck in the field.

Things were just normal for a bit. One cool October day, after we got all the animals fed and the water passed to each pig pen, it was time to leave the farm. As the sun was going down, Mom turned the key over in the truck, but it did not start. We were five miles from home, it was getting dark, and now we were going to have to walk home down winding gravel roads in complete darkness. We took turns carrying our little brothers on our back because they were tired of walking and were being fussy. Of course, there was no one we could look to for help. When we got home, Wayne was still not there.

As the arguing and fighting at home continued to worsen, Cheryl had finally found some happiness within herself. She had Michael, and I was happy for her. I could see a sparkle in her eyes that I hadn't seen in a long time. She finally had found someone who cared about her the way that she deserved. They went to homecoming together, and she was so excited. I couldn't wait until she got home from the dance so that she could tell me how it was and what songs they played. I could get some sense of enjoyment from her happiness. Music became a big part of our lives as many hours of the day were spent in our room, listening to music, dancing, and imagining taking ourselves to places where we wished we could be. We spent as much time out of sight because if not, we were being used like his personal slaves. Wayne would just sit in his chair, watch tv, and spout off orders: "Make me a cup of coffee, and put a cap of milk in it." "Hand me the remote." "Go make me a sandwich." "Go see what your mom wants." "Close that blind a little bit." It was ridiculous! This man could not do anything for himself.

One cold afternoon, Cheryl and I were outside talking, and she told me that they were planning on going to the lake to stay at the cabin. She said that Wayne had told her that Michael was coming. He had gotten close with Michael because Wayne used him on the farm as well. I think it was just to see if Cheryl would ever tell Michael anything. I told them I was going too because I didn't let Cheryl go anywhere without me. Wayne was mad that I said I was going to go. He said that they would have to pick up Michael along the way. I told her I was running inside to use the bathroom quickly because that was a long drive. As I was in the bathroom, I heard the truck start up. I tried to hurry as fast as I could. As I ran out the door, I could see the truck pulling out of the driveway and onto the street.

The Unforgivable

I began crying, "Where are they going? I told you I was going too!" I began to look around frantically for Cheryl. "Where is she?" Mom told me that they had already left. I was so mad. "He knew I wanted to go!" I yelled. I went into my room and slammed the door. My heart was racing. I was scared. I was scared for her. We had never broken our pact since that day. Now, I felt like I had let her down. In my heart, I felt something was wrong. I lay on the couch in the living room that night. Lying there with my eyes wide open, I was unable to sleep. Something was wrong, and I could feel it.

By 2:00 a.m., I heard the truck pull into the driveway. Then I heard someone wiggling the back doorknob. I jumped up and ran to open the door. I saw my sister standing there with her head down. As I opened the door, she pushed past me and walked to the bedroom. Wayne came into the house after her.

Mama came from out of the bedroom, where she had been sleeping, and said, "What are ya'll doing back?" He told her he was missing home and decided to come on back.

I went into the bedroom. Cheryl sat on the edge of the bed. I could hear her sniffling.

I asked her, "What happened?"

Allie woke up and sat up on the side of the bed and asked what was going on. Cheryl then told us that they didn't go get Michael. Wayne told her that Michael wasn't ready and that their friend Christian was going to pick Michael up and meet them up there. When they got up there, no one was there. After a while of waiting, no one showed up. She said that Wayne had started to drink, so she went to go to bed. Wayne then went into the room where she was. She closed her eyes and pretended to be asleep, but she could see that all he had on was his underwear. He got into the bed and lay next to her. He started touching her private areas and tried to get her to have sex with him.

When she tried to get away from him, he hit her and pulled her back. She made her way out to the truck after getting away from him, and he followed her. She insisted that she was going home. As she tried to run away, he grabbed her and threw her into the truck. He continued to hit her in the face as he drove back, and he told her he could just throw her in the lake and tell our mom that she ran off with some niggers. She was so scared. She thought he was going to kill her.

I turned on the bathroom light so I could see her face, and then I saw the blood running down her face and onto her already blood-stained shirt. Her lips were swollen and busted. As I helped her clean up, I told her not to worry, that I would take care of it in the morning. That night, I lay in bed, and she lay beside me. I cried. I felt like I had let her down again, and I was supposed to protect her from this ever happening again. She knew I had no fear of him and that I would make sure that Mom knew what happened.

As the sun glared through the bedroom window the following morning, I heard Mom in the kitchen. I called her into the bedroom and handed her the bloody shirt and had her look at Cheryl's face. Mom asked her what happened.

I told her, "That son of a bitch has done it again. That is why they came back. He tried to rape her, and then he beat the hell out of her."

She replied with, "Oh, did he now?" She stormed into the bedroom, where he still lay sleeping, and began to yell at him. "What did you do? What did you do? Huh? You did it again, huh? So why did you come back? What the hell happened?" My sisters and I got our little brothers and went outside so that they wouldn't have to hear the fighting.

This turned out to be an all-day fight. Periodically, we could hear him acting as if he was crying, stating he didn't know what was wrong with him and that he didn't know why he did it. Hours passed, and darkness came. Why was he not leaving? Mom promised us he was leaving, yet he remained. We finally fell asleep as we waited for something to happen.

The next day, Mom called us all into the living room without him, and she told us he was not our dad and that we didn't have to listen to him anymore. I asked her why he was not leaving, and she told me that I didn't have to worry about it anymore. I asked her why she was allowing him to continue to do this and get away with it. I told her if he kept doing it to Cheryl, he was probably doing stuff to Bub because he was still having him sleep in the same bed. Mom made the comment that she had thought about that too and that she wouldn't doubt it. That situation was strange as

Mom had stopped sleeping with Wayne and Bub was sleeping in the same bed with him. Bub wouldn't know to say anything because of his mental intellect. He only said and did what he was told to do.

The thing was that Mom had no answers. He told her that he didn't know why he did it. This was the moment that my heart grew cold and bitter. The one person in my life that was supposed to protect us was walking away from us and allowing this to happen. She had left our real dad because he was abusive to her, but now she was allowing another man to be abusive to her children. What sense did this make? Maybe now that the abuse was not directed at her, it was easier to turn and look the other way. This was the point where my emotion switch was turned completely off.

Chapter 5

Things really began to spiral out of control. The fighting turned into a daily routine. The hate that he had for me after I told Mom about what he had done began to show. The hate that I had for him I also wanted to show. I will say that from that point, I was no angel. The resentment that I had for him was astounding and would only grow stronger. He looked for reasons to fight. If Mom said I could go somewhere or do something, he would say no. Of course, I would fight it. After all, Mom said that we didn't have to listen to him anymore. I would quickly remind him that he was not my father and remind him that I had not forgotten what he had done to Cheryl. He would quickly hit me in the face or grab my jaw and shake my face, telling me I was going to listen to him. I would just stare at him. Mom just stood by and listened, only intervening if things were being broken or if the punches were loud enough.

One night, Joker and Wayne got into a fight. He punched Joker hard in the eye and began to choke him. Joker threw him on the floor, and then he ran out the door and told Wayne he would be back to kill him. Mom and Wayne blamed my brother for the incident, stating that he was on drugs. The next day, Joker came home to get clothes. His eye was swollen shut and bloody. We couldn't even see the white of his eye. He was working at Ramey's, the local grocery, and I was sure that someone would call and report it or question it. But no one ever did. I began to see less and less of Joker after that. I couldn't blame him. If I could be gone, I would too. That was when Joker went down the path of selling drugs and using drugs to provide for himself and cover up the emotional scars that were so deep within. Not long after that began, my brother moved into his own place.

One afternoon, I came home very excited. I was asked to stay all night at a friend's house. Mom told me that I could go. I was so happy. I was finally going somewhere like other kids. I had my skates on and went inside to get my things to get ready to go.

Then Wayne said, "Get ready. We are going to the hog farm."

I told him that I wasn't going, that I was going to my friend's house. He told me that I wasn't going to my friend's house.

As I stood up from the bed, I said to him, "Mom said I don't have to go."

Within seconds, I felt his fist pound the left side of my temple. Everything went black as I flew backward across the bed. The ringing in my ear was very intense. Mom was in the bathroom, and she heard the noise.

I heard her yell, "Why did you have to hit her?"

I just lay there, still unable to hear anything out of my ear besides ringing, and seeing nothing but light and darkness.

Then she turned to me and says, "If you would just shut your smart-ass mouth, he wouldn't have done that."

I was so mad I couldn't even think. I jumped up from the floor in a drunken stupor from the blow and went for the first thing I could get my hands on—his head. I wanted this man to feel some kind of pain. The metal box fan was the first thing that I could see sitting on my dresser. I grabbed it and hurled it at his head as hard as I could. He then turned and came toward me again. His fist wrapped around my throat, and he squeezed tight. At the same time, he told me he didn't have to put up with me anymore. I sat there as he choked me, trying to get free. After a few minutes, he decided to let go.

Then I looked him in his eyes and told him, "You can't hurt me. I haven't forgotten what you have done, and I do not have to listen to you."

As he headed toward me again, I got around him and ran out the back door. I ran as fast as my legs would take me, tears streaming down my face. I didn't know what was worse—the beatings or the fact that my mother would blame me for it. She was not there to protect me. I continued to walk up and down side streets just to be alone, honestly wishing I was dead and would not have to deal with this on a daily basis.

After about an hour, I walked up the alley street behind our house and could see that the truck was gone. I headed back to the house to see if the coast was clear. Mom and Wayne had left to go to the hog farm. My sisters were there. I was fed up. As I looked at myself in the mirror and saw the swelling around my temple, I grew even angrier. I told my sisters that I'd had enough, that I wasn't putting up with this anymore.

I told them, "Come on, we're leaving. We need to hurry up before they come back."

We walked down the street to my uncle Joe's house, and I told him everything that had happened that day and about the physical and the sexual abuse toward my sister. My uncle called the police. For once, I felt like someone was listening to us. It felt like we sat in the police station for hours, telling them our side of the story, talking to children services and police officers. Then an officer brought in a suitcase that I knew was one that my mom had brought. He said that she brought us some clothes and that we would be staying with Grandma until things could be sorted out.

Chapter 6

We had spent very little time around our grandma growing up, so this was definitely awkward for us. Our family seemed like the black sheep of the family. Our cousins were always at Grandma's, staying the night, going out on the boat, and having holiday dinners; but we were always excluded. I was not sure why that was, but that was how it was. Going to live with Grandma was something new. Being in a home environment without fighting was going to be a change. Hell, being in a home that was so exquisitely furnished was a change.

My grandma took us to the eye doctor and to the dentist for the first time. I remember being in school in the second grade and not being able to see the chalkboard. I always prayed that my seat would be in the front so I wouldn't have to squint so hard to see. But telling my mom that I couldn't see got me nowhere. It was if she didn't believe me, like I was making it up. So I just got by the best way I could. If the teacher asked me the answer to the problem on the board, I would guess, and when I guessed the wrong answer because I couldn't see, everyone would laugh because they thought I didn't know the answer. The truth was, I couldn't see the problem to know what the answer was. So I just sat there as they laughed at me, and I waited for the teacher to go on to the next student. Sometimes she would do so immediately, but sometimes she would accuse me of not paying attention, as I was already in the seventh grade.

We lived with Grandma for about a month. Then came court day. Before court, we had to meet with the juvenile officer, Bill Myers. As we went in, he asked us to have a seat. He talked to us one at a time. As I sat there, he asked questions about my grandma and how things were going. I told him that things were going well. He then told Allie and me that we were not going back to Grandma's and that Cheryl was going to be placed in foster care. When we asked why, he stated that Grandma was unable to take care of us. I couldn't understand this reasoning. We were old enough to take care of ourselves. We were not babies. I told him that I was not going back home. I was not going to go back to live like that. He then asked me what I would like to do. I told him I didn't care. I just didn't want to go back there to be around Wayne.

Myers then began to ask me questions about my aunt Jill who lived in Arkansas. He stated that maybe I needed to go live there. I was upset because I had not been around her either. I didn't even know her; she was like a stranger to me. And he was wanting to take me away from what friends I had at school and my siblings and move me to the house of a relative whom I had maybe seen once or twice in my life. Allie decided to go live with her friend in Tennessee.

As Bill Meyers sat across from me, he looked at me and said, "Well, maybe you just have a smart mouth." He then decided that I would go live with my other aunt Georgia who lived in the same town. My aunt had my little cousins at home, which I had been around more than anyone else so that seemed like it would be fine. I was scared because my aunt had not lived a stable life. She had her fair share of abusive relationships and drug problems. But anything had to be better than going back home.

It was that day that Cheryl was placed in foster care. We were all split apart, something that we never thought would happen. I would find out years later that my grandma had placed a call to my dad and informed him about the situation. She had told my dad that he needed to come get us because we were "running around with niggers and not listening." This was the story that our mom had given to Grandma. Up to this point, we had probably only seen Grandma a handful of times. This was the reason our dad showed up at the courthouse that day, and we hadn't seen him in at least ten years.

The days at my aunt's started off good. I spent the days after school with my little cousins outside, riding bikes or jumping rope. My little cousin Tara and I used to sit up at night in bed and talk to each other until one of us fell asleep. We used to look out of the window and watch the cars drive by or the other kids walking back and forth across the parking lot. We were shut inside, not really allowed to talk to anybody. My aunt would ask me every other day if I was ready to go back home. She would say, "Don't you miss your mom? She wants you to come back home." The sad thing was, I did miss my mom. She wasn't the reason that I did not want to be there. I was mad at her for choosing Wayne over us. I talked to my mom a couple of times during the first few weeks of being there, and she would ask me how things were going. Honestly, it was a place to live. I wasn't happy. I was separated from my brothers and sisters. But it was better than what I had to deal with at home.

It became obvious that my aunt really didn't want me to be there. She began to talk to me like I was her hired help. She would call me names and tell me to get in the kitchen and clean it up. I would wash the dishes, mop and sweep the floor, and clean the rest of the house. I really tried my best to make her like me or at least not mind that I was there. I didn't expect to live there for nothing. After all, she got my social security check, and I watched her kids while she ran around with different men. Even this was nothing in comparison to what I had already had to deal with in my life. This was easy. But why did she not like me? After all, how could I expect her to love me when she didn't even know me or even try to know me?

As I got off the bus one day, I saw my things sitting on the porch. My heart sank. As I walked into the door, I saw her sitting on the couch. She said, "You are going back home today." I was at a loss for words. Of course, she waited until she received my social security check, and now she was putting me out. She didn't even have the heart to take me back herself. She called her ex-husband, whom I barely knew, to pick me up and take me back. Without explanation, I was returning to the hell I had left two months ago. I wasn't sure if Mom knew that I was coming back or not.

As he pulled up in front of the house, I felt a feeling that I couldn't explain. I knew that things were going to be much worse than before. He dropped me off at the house, and I gathered my few things from the car and walked toward the front door. Mom opened the front door and let me in. She stated, "You're back. There won't be any of that smartass mouth this time." Disgust and frustration from the fact that I was back were clearly written on her face. At this point, I was beyond frustrated at the system. I now had the mentality that I just did not care anymore. I was not going to take his or her shit anymore. I was in the mindset of "It's going to be me or him, but I ain't going down without a fight."

I was so depressed and honestly thought of many ways to end my misery. He would find ways to pick arguments just to get me to react. It was always either the dishes were not clean enough, the kitchen wasn't clean enough, or the music was too loud. It didn't matter. He would always find a reason to yell at me. I began to smoke weed around this time just to get rid of some of the feelings that I was having. I also began cutting myself just to find another form of pain to feel. The adrenaline rush from the pain somewhere else cleared my mind temporarily.

After Allie realized that I was back at home, she came back. It was the happiest day of my life. Finally, I had one of my sisters back. We didn't get to see Cheryl. We couldn't talk to her on the phone or anything. At this point, we were not allowed to talk to anybody on the phone. We began to just get out and walk around town just to get away and have time to ourselves to talk about other things besides how to survive in that hellhole. Where was help from the community? Not one person stopped to ask any questions in the many times we walked outside. We could only cry in silence.

One summer afternoon, I was in my room, listening to music. I was not allowed to close my bedroom door, which was right next to the living room, where Wayne would sit and watch TV all day. He began to yell, "Turn that nigger shit down." I told him that it was not too loud, that no matter how loud it was, it was always going to be too loud to him because he wouldn't let me shut the door. He then stood up and went into the bedroom, yelling at me. And of course, I yelled back. Within seconds, I felt the thud of his fist against the right side of my head. He continued to punch me in the face and head. I heard my sister yell at my mom from the kitchen, "If you don't go get him off her, I will." Everything went black. The next thing I remember was him leaving the room.

I was sick and tired of hiding my injuries to my lips, cheekbones, and nose from his beatings. There were times when I would sit and plan ways to kill him so I wouldn't have to deal with this anymore. I thought of how hard I would have to bash in his skull as he lay in bed at night to kill him. Something had to give, or one of us was going to die.

There was a time when I walked into his room, where he was lying asleep, while I held an iron skillet in my hand. I walked up to the side of the bed. I could hear him breathing. The only light in the room was the night light on the wall on the other side of the bed. As I pulled the skillet back, ready to drive it into his face, I saw a shadow come across the night light, and I saw that my mom was on the bed next to him. She sat straight up in bed, looking at me. With the skillet in the air, I looked over at her and saw her glaring at me. She put her finger to her lips in the "Shhh" position, and she reached up and touched my arm to pull it down. I then turned around and walked out of the room.

Maybe that was her way of saving my life that night. Because at that moment, I did not care what the consequences would be. I was living in a world of hell, and the system just did not care. Teachers at school never asked any questions, people in public just stared but never said anything, and no one came to our defense. Even though I felt in my soul that this was not how kids were supposed to be treated, the fact that no one did anything made me question my thoughts.

A social worker began coming to the house for home visits after I came back home, but that was a joke. She just sat there and jotted on her paper while Mom and Wayne continued to talk about how much of a disrespectful child I was. I spoke up one time to mention the beating that I had gotten from him, and he denied it. Mom stood by his side and backed him up, telling the social worker that I was lying about it. Why did the social worker never ask me any questions? The conversations were always between them, while I sat there being labeled as the problem. Of course, nothing happened, and things only got worse after the social worker left, so at that point, I didn't bother to say anything else.

How could someone see the signs of the abuse going on in this house and still do absolutely nothing? It was unreal to me. Pretty soon, the social worker stopped coming by. They had failed me once. This time was no different. Allie and I used to sit out on the swing in the yard, and I would tell her that once I left that hellhole, I would never return no matter what. I didn't care if I would be homeless—I meant it. I sat there and thought of the times that he choked me until I almost passed out or the times when he would clutch my jaw so hard, I thought it would snap. I hated it here, and I was never coming back once I got away from it. There were many nights of being choked and dragged around the house like a ragdoll until I could get loose from him. It was always predictable.

Then I would run out the door and keep running. The wind hit me in the face while my tears streamed down my face. Not one damn person stopped to ask me if I was okay. But one day, as I ran down the street, crying so hard I could barely catch my breath, there was one person who stopped and asked me what was wrong, and he had always held a place in my heart through the years. He was a neighbor from behind us, and he was African American. He knew it would be a big problem if he was caught talking to me, but he didn't care. He pulled up next to me and told me to get in. I didn't hesitate as I got into the passenger side of his car. I told him that we had a fight, and he was aware of what went on in that house.

We talked to him periodically but had to do so in secret because they didn't like us associating with black people. He was much older than me. He was Joker's's age. As I sat in his car, he asked me what he could do, and I told him to just get me away from there. As he drove around town in silence, every now and then, he looked over at me to make sure that I was still okay. It was nice to be around someone who actually cared, and he was definitely willing to do something to put a stop to it. But I didn't want to bring my troubles to him. My tears were from the betrayal and hurt my mother caused me. She was supposed to protect me, but she was allowing this man to beat the life right out of me.

I hated the police department, the children's services, and the court system. This man was never charged or held accountable for the sexual abuse to my sister. He never stood a day in court; much less questioned. Cheryl passed her lie detector test, and he refused to take one, but it went nowhere. What kind of system removes a child from a home due to suspected sexual abuse but leaves the other children there? We were literally told that due to the accusation of sexual abuse with my sister, that was why they had to remove her. But I guess the physical abuse didn't matter to them. We were not protected from the physical abuse that we encountered daily, and they knew about it. My respect and hope for help from anyone out of this situation was gone. I knew the only way I was going to get away from this was on my own.

Chapter 7

I made a few friends growing up. They knew about what I went through at home, and they were always there to listen when I needed to talk. Holidays would come around, and kids at school would talk about what they were going to do or where they were going to go on vacation. I used to envy them because that was not the kind of life that I lived. I dreaded the coming of those long breaks from school because I knew that meant I would be where I didn't want to be.

We did not get Easter baskets or birthday presents. On Halloween, we would make our own costumes and go trick-or-treating all over town, only for Wayne to take all our candies, put them in a big bowl, and tell us that we could only get it when he said so or after he got what he wanted out of it. Thanksgiving brought the best of my mom's cooking, but it always ended in a huge fight or argument. Because of the food, though, we looked forward to it. The arguments always start because of us not cleaning things up right or not doing it well enough or because we were being too loud while he slept in the living room. It didn't matter. He would always find a reason to make anything good turn into something bad.

I used to wonder why in school they asked us what we were thankful for. Other kids would say their mom or dad. I would make something up, so I could fit in with everyone else. But deep down, I felt as if I had nothing to be thankful for. I would always wonder if there were kids that were going through the same thing as myself. If this was what life was like, it wasn't worth it. Every day was a struggle. It would just depend on what he could think of when he woke up.

As I got a little older, I only had a few classmates I considered to be real friends. Those were the ones that I considered to be loyal, respectful, and accepted me for who I was. I considered myself to have a free, clear mind from the judgment of others. It came naturally to me, and I expected others to feel the same way toward me. Unfortunately, that was not the way it was. I had a lot of African American friends. As a matter of fact, most of them were. Although I wasn't allowed to hang out with them outside of school or talk about them at home, they knew my situation, and we still bonded.

In New Madrid, a small Southern town, dating someone outside your race was not accepted by most, and they truly believed that dating someone of another race was wrong. Wayne would tell me over and over that the Bible stated it was a sin. I would argue about the subject many times, telling him to prove it, and of course, I was never produced the scripture in the Bible that stated that. Even at the age of thirteen, there was no way that I could or would accept the fact that God said or believed that dating someone of another race was a sin. Every single person was created by God, yet Wayne wanted me to believe that I was supposed to look at a race other than myself differently.

I started to question my faith in God after hearing that so many times. I would ask myself, "If that is what God wants or says, then what kind of God, was he? Who or what type of person would I be to follow him?" Choosing to go against what many of the people around you believe is a hard choice to make, especially when it means losing family and friends and being hated by many. But I had never been a follower. I stood firm in the choices that I made, and I didn't rely on others' opinions to decide what was right.

I started going to church on Wednesdays and Sundays. I loved being around others who was kind and loving. It was something that I was lacking at home, and I needed to learn more about God and his legacy to people. I needed to find out if what I was being told to believe was true. I met some new friends, and honestly, church was my escape. I looked forward to those days every week. It was the only thing to look forward to.

The church bus driver, Steve, knew what was going on at home. He would come get me early and take me out to eat after church just to keep me out longer. He made comments every now and then that things weren't right. I knew that he had talked to the people of the church about it because when it came time for church camp or things that cost money, they would always pay my way through so that I could go. They never even asked questions. I knew they probably looked at me like I was an unfortunate child who lacked money and new clothes as I still wore hand-me-downs from my sister at this point.

I had met some good friends at church, and at least while I was with them, I felt like a normal teenager, although I would often think about how much better they had it than me with their name brand clothes, cars, and money. I would dream about when the time would come that things would be different for me if I made it that long. All good things must come to an end though. When Wayne realized how happy going to church made me, he used that against me as my punishment to everything. If I talked too loudly, did not move fast enough, or didn't pour his coffee when he said to, my privilege of going to church was taken away.

I performed in my first Christmas pageant at that church. My friends looked out into the crowd to see their family, but I knew I had no one to look for. No one ever came. Standing in my white dress with a sparkling silver glitter halo, so proud of myself for the part that I played. The proud moment soon faded as I remembered no one was there to congratulate me like the others. After a couple of years, the time finally came that Wayne stopped me from going back to church. He would call them hypocrites and say that I cared more about them than I did anything else. He wasn't wrong about that part. I am not sure if it was because of his pure hatred for me or because of fear that his dark secrets would be revealed.

My childhood home was not one that I was proud of. Inside it held a dark, deep stigma. Little did I know that it would continue to follow me throughout my life. Our home was not a happy home. I cannot tell you that there were not good times, but I will tell you that the bad times outweighed the good. Allie and I had developed a close relationship, as we were the only two children left in the home that did not belong to my stepfather. At this point, there was no communication between our sister in foster care and very little with our older brother. We would go for walks, sit out in the grass, and talk for hours about places we wanted to go to or about things that we wanted to do once we left. One thing I knew for sure is that, once I left, I was not coming back no matter what the situation was. There was nothing on earth that could bring me back to this.

I would often sit and wonder why my mom was the way she was and why she allowed these things to go on. She would have her moments of laughing and smiling, but it was never with Wayne around. Now that I look back, I feel that she was like that because she was afraid that he would get mad if she was nice to us because we were not worthy of being nice to. I heard some of my friends telling their mom that they loved them and they would hug. It felt awkward for me because I had never heard those words and couldn't remember the last time that my mom hugged me. Did she not really love me? Was I just existing to her now because I had to be?

Chapter 8

In the spring of 1995, my sister and I were out walking on the levee. The levee was the most peaceful place in the world to me. It was very close to the river, and I could hear the wind blow loud enough to drown everything else out. The water seemed like it flowed forever, and looking out, I could see an island in the middle and sometimes imagined what it would be like to live there, away from everything and everybody. Allie had begun talking to a guy named Ryan from out of town. She had met him through her friend Megan. We would meet him up on the levee away from everyone so that we wouldn't get caught. We would get in his car and just drive around or just park there and watch the river.

One day, he brought a friend with him—Greg. I instantly thought he was the cutest boy I had ever seen. He was so sweet and funny but also very shy. We began hanging out together as much as we could under the circumstances, as we knew that if we got caught with them, we would be in serious trouble. We stuck to back roads and the levee. He was quiet and amazingly handsome to me. Love at first sight—was it true? Did it really exist? We enjoyed our time together by talking and laughing with each other. He had a way of making me forget the hell that awaited me when I was away from him. When I was away from him, all I could think about was the next time I would be with him. He had that way about him that made me smile.

At times, we would sit and look into each other's eyes and never say a word but seemed to read each other's thoughts. We spent as much time as possible together. Greg lived in another town and was a couple years older than me, so we were unable to see each other every day. The sawmill became our hangout place. We would park there and walk around through the stacks of lumber under the streetlight, looking down at our shadows in the darkness so close to each other. Finally, on one occasion, as we stood there facing each other, hand in hand, we looked into each other's eyes. At that moment, we both leaned in toward each other, and our lips touched. I could feel butterflies in my stomach. Every ounce of fear left my soul. Within his arms, I felt safe. Everything felt so right. At that moment, he washed away all the chaos in my life.

I had never had this feeling before. Greg was the one I wanted and needed in my life. He was what was missing. The only problem was the fact that I knew my family would not accept him because he was African American. I knew this would be a battle that I would not win and that I could not tell my family about him. Therefore, our relationship remained a secret out of protection of myself and him.

I was able to talk about him to my friends at school, and things just felt so normal. But then some of the other boys would laugh and say, "Your mama and daddy ain't fixing to let you be with a nigger!" It used to infuriate me when they said that. Even though they would laugh like they were cracking jokes, I knew that they knew how it was at home. It was embarrassing to me, but little did they know that I was not one of the stand-down kids like everyone else. I didn't care what other people thought of me. I didn't care how others felt about me.

Allie and I finally were allowed to go stay the night with Cheryl at the foster home. I am not sure why mom finally gave in, but she did. Seeing Cheryl for the first time after so long was so exciting. I had missed her so much. She showed us her room and took us on their four wheelers, and they took us horseback riding. I was honestly truly jealous that she was living a great life while we were still in a life of hell at home. But we didn't talk much about that while we were there. We just soaked it all in and tried to catch up on things we had missed about each other since we had been apart.

Greg called us that night while we were there. They were in town at a payphone, and he just wanted to say hi. Although I tried to get him to come over, he was respectful and didn't want to get me in trouble, so he didn't. The following day, we went back home, and that was the last time we were allowed to go back.

On Halloween night, Allie and I decided that we were going to meet up with the guys to hang out. I guess that we had gotten comfortable in our routine of doing things that we failed to pay attention to the details. They would always ride by with the music blaring, and we always knew it was them because no one else in town would come through our neighborhood with music that loud. That would be our signal to wait a few minutes and then leave to meet them.

After the sun went down and everyone else was out trick-or-treating, I heard the beat of the music as they passed in front of our house. We knew they were close. We left the house and headed to our meet-up spot. We got in with them a few blocks away from the house. We drove up on the levee and decided we would park there and get out to take a walk.

As we got out of the car, Greg held my hand, and we walked next to the boat ramp. I felt the warmth of his body as he put his arms around me while the chilly air blew around us. We stood there in silence, just the sound of his heartbeat in my ear. Then I looked up and saw headlights coming down the levee. My heart started to beat faster, but Greg never moved but instead held me close to his chest.

I thought to myself, Please don't let that be Mom.

As the car approached, I realized that it was a police car. Greg took my hand as the police officers got out of the car and started to walk closer to us.

They shined their lights on us, and one of them said, "What are you kids doing down here?"

I replied, "Just hanging out."

The officer told us to walk up to the picnic tables, and one told Greg and Ryan to take a seat on the bench.

The other officer called me over away from Greg, and he said to me, "Does your mother know you are here?"

I said, "No."

He then asked me, "Was he trying to hurt you?"

I laughed and stated, "No, he is my boyfriend."

He then replied, "Does your mom know that you are with them?"

Before I could say anything else, I saw another set of headlights coming down the levee and heard the hum of a very familiar truck. It was my mother.

As she pulled the truck over and got out, she walked down the levee and instantly started yelling, "Get in the fucking truck! I've had enough of this shit!"

I looked over at Greg and mouthed, "I'm sorry."

Tears began to fill my eyes as I walked away. I did not realize this would be the last time that I would look into his eyes or feel his arms around me. I didn't know I would never get the chance to tell him how much he really meant to me. My heart was shattered. I was embarrassed and hurt at the way my mom acted toward him—as if he were nobody, as if he didn't have feelings too.

Mom walked over toward the benches where Greg and Ryan were sitting and yelled, "Keep your black asses away from my daughters!"

As we began to drive off, the police remained talking to Greg and Ryan. I tried to drown out her yelling.

In the car, Mom kept on yelling, "How would you like it if you got put in a girls' home? That is where they put young-ass girls like you who run around with niggers. That's what I should do with you!"

The beating of that black leather belt that night came with force and fury. The number of swings of that leather against my skin was uncountable. I was so mad. I refused to show my stepfather that he was hurting me. I held the tears back, and with each swing, I just glared at him. He swung until he was too tired to swing it anymore.

The rest of that night was a blur. I could not think about anything or anyone but Greg. I knew seeing him again would be next to impossible. Mom and Wayne changed our phone number at that time and never told us what it was. They were afraid that we would give it to Greg and Ryan. When they left the house, they unplugged the phone so we couldn't use it, and they threatened us if we dared to leave while they were gone.

New Madrid Levee Riverfront- The last place I would see the love of my life before being torn apart by racial discrimination in 1995. It continues to hold a sentimental place in my heart burdened by anger and hurt.

My life from that point on began to spiral out of control. As days passed, I continued to try to contact Greg through calls from payphones and even letters, which I sent to his grandma's. I sent him a picture of me in hopes that he would not forget me. I apologized that he had to go through that. I never got a response. My heart was broken as I was unsure if he was mad at me for what happened that night. I could not do anything but think the worst. I was embarrassed by the reaction my mom had toward him and was hurt by the thought of him not wanting to see me again. I was beaten and threatened of being placed in a girls' home just because I had fallen in love with someone of a different color. The thing was, we were not different at all. On the inside, we shared the same thoughts, feelings, and dreams as anyone else.

Many nights, I would cry myself to sleep, feeling like my entire world was crumbling down around me. The one person in my life who made me feel safe, accepted me, and I enjoyed being with was taken away from me without any warning. It was a chapter in my life that would be left open without any explanation and many unanswered questions and emotions. One day, while sitting in class, I wrote him a final letter. I didn't have his name on it because I didn't want any trouble from it. When the school bell rang for the next class, I was called down to the principal's office.

As I walked into Mr. Hines's office, he told me to have a seat. He laid the letter on his desk. It must have dropped from my book bag while I was changing classes. He asked me if it was mine, and I said yes. He then asked me who it was written for. I couldn't tell him who it was really written for because I didn't want to get Greg into trouble. So I told him it was another boy who had a crush on me.

Much to my surprise, he asked me if my mother knew that I dated black boys. I told him that yes, she did. Then he talked to me about the rules against writing love letters in school, which by the way made no sense at all to me. Honestly, this was only a problem because it was a letter written to a black boy. Then my mom walked into the office. This asshole literally called my mom so he could be the first to inform her that I was dating a black boy. You have got to be kidding me! If he only knew the hell I was fixing to go through at home because she knew exactly whom the letter was for.

Thank you, Mr. Hines, for being so supportive and making it known that you don't view black boys the same as white boys. I'm not really sure why I thought you would be different from everyone else. After all, New Madrid County was one of the last schools in Missouri to end segregation years after it was ended by law. (They definitely still viewed themselves invincible to the law.) But thanks again, Mr. Hines, for igniting the fire for me once again at home.

Chapter 9

Life began to change for me—and not for the better. I began to smoke weed regularly. Hell, who were they to judge? I was getting the weed from their friend who was at the house every day. I mean the guy was much older than my sister and me, but they really tried to push him onto Allie. She was not going to let that happen. They questioned the type of friends I had, yet this was the type of people they brought around to "date their daughter." He was white—that was the difference to them.

I began to drink frequently as thoughts of rage and hate toward my mother and this man who called himself my stepfather began to grow stronger. I resented them for making me live like this. How come I could not be like the other kids? How come I could not have a mother who told me she loved me or hugged me good night? Instead, she could barely look at me. I was only acknowledged when I was being yelled at or beaten by a man whom she allowed to beat me. She never attended any school concerts, functions, and parent–teacher conferences. I never resented the fact that we were poor. I resented the things that many children took for granted. Most kids wanted new clothes, shoes, or video games, but I just wanted acknowledgement that I was not a worthless child and that I mattered to somebody.

I began to put all my efforts into school. This was going to be my way out. This was an escape from it all. At school, the teachers would tell me how great of a job I did on a paper. I made almost straight As in school. I was finally allowed to go back to church on Wednesdays and Sundays as well. I surrounded myself with people who cared about me for a change. It was times like these, I could finally see just how wrong things were at home. I was able to see how children were supposed to be treated. I was jealous. I resented many of them because I had never experienced that kind of life.

It was at church that I met a lady who worked at a children's home in East Prairie. She asked me one day if I was related to Cheryl, and my eyes lit up. I told her that she was my sister and that I had not seen her for a long time. Obviously, since she knew my sister, she knew the history of my family. She took me under her wing. Every Sunday, after church, she would take me home with her, and we would go to the children's home so I could spend the afternoon with my sister. Even though she knew that this was against the rules, she made it happen for me. I had missed my sister so much. It felt like things were changing so fast. She was growing up and making a life for herself. She had a boyfriend now and was happy. I was happy for her, but I was resentful because I was stuck living the same nightmare repeatedly.

It was not long after I began going back to church that they began to use that against me once again. If they were mad at me for anything, he would always stop me from going to church. He would tell me I was a hypocrite because I went to church even though I liked niggers. He said, "I wonder how them church people would look at you if they knew what you were?" This continued until I finally just stopped going. I honestly thought that they were afraid because I was closer to the people at church and they were afraid that I might say something about the way I was treated at home.

But at this point, I would not tell anybody anything. What was the point? They had already let me down before, so why even bother? Why would I put myself through the embarrassment and torture of spilling my heart out to other people when they do nothing? After all, if people could look at me and still not know that something was wrong within these walls, they were not looking hard enough. Visits with my sister ended at the same time I stopped going to church. I figured something would eventually bring us back together again. She would soon reach legal age and was planning to get married. I was happy that at least one of us was getting something positive out of life. Meanwhile, the struggle at home continued.

One day, Wayne's friend brought his son to the house. I was fourteen years old hanging out with a nineteen-year-old man. They sat and talked about how we looked cute together and that I needed to make him my boyfriend. I told them and his mother no, that it was not going to happen because I was not into him like that. He was nice, but he was too old for me. I did not like him that way. That was guy number one they were trying to set me up with.

Then there came the checkout guy at the grocery store. He bagged our groceries every time we went. Mom always talked to him, and he was always acting weird around me. He was twenty. He talked about how cute I was. Then one night, he asked if I wanted to go for a ride with him when he got off work. Mom spoke up and said, "Yeah, that's fine. She will go. Just come and pick her up at the house." At this point, it did not feel right, but I honestly did not care. I was grasping at straws to find a way out of there for any given amount of time.

He picked me up at the house, and he asked me what I wanted to do. I told him I did not care. Little did I know that he had other things in mind. As he made his way past the high school, my heart sank as he turned down the gravel road. I figured at this point that it was too late to do anything because there was nowhere to run and no one to hear me scream. So he pulled up to a small turnoff on the side of the road, which put us on the outskirts of a field, and he opened the door. I asked him what he was doing getting out, and he told me to get out, that he wanted to show me something.

As I walked to the front of the car, he spread a blanket on the ground and grabbed my hand and told me to lie down.

I was thinking to myself, "Is this really happening?" I complied against my better judgement.

He asked me if I had ever had sex before, and I told him no.

He said, "That's good. I will take it easy."

I thought, Great. I am really going to lose my virginity to a grocery store checkout guy whom I do not find attractive, much less know anything about, and on the ground in the middle of a field.

As I lay down on the ground, he pulled my shorts down. I closed my eyes, praying for it to be over. As I felt him push his penis toward me, I began to cry.

"Stop. Please, just stop!" I cried.

He raised up and looked down at me and stated, "Are you serious?" I began to push him away from me, and he said, "I thought you wanted to."

I asked him, "During what part of our small talk we had did I tell you I wanted to sleep with you?"

I got up and pulled my shorts up, then got in the car. He threw the blanket in the backseat and got in, slamming the door. The whole ride home was in complete silence.

As he pulled up in front of my house, he said, "Do not tell anybody about this."

Shame, embarrassment, and insecurity pretty much described the way I felt at that time in my life.

And as it turned out, he was a brother to a friend of mine, and he told me not to tell her what happened. When I got back home, I called my friend.

She laughed and said, "I can't believe you slept with my brother!"

I told her that I didn't, and she told me that he had said that we had sex. I informed her that it did not go down as he had told her. Then we never talked about it again.

The next afternoon, after school, I walked to her apartment with her. She lived with her dad. She said that we were going to get some weed to smoke. She ran in real quick, and then she came out with at least an ounce of weed. We walked to the park and sat out there, talking and laughing while we smoked. Then we decided to walk to the village where a good friend of mine lived. He knew my situation at home, and even though he liked me, he never pushed the issue. We were just friends. I began to get a little nervous as for what seemed like hours passed, we sat in the apartment, getting high.

She, of course, went in the back room to have sex with a random guy that came up. I didn't understand why she did that kind of stuff, but it wasn't anything new or uncommon with her. We were friends because, like me, she had begun to date outside the white race as well. That was pretty much the only thing we had in common. As we left their apartment that night and began walking back in the dark, she knew she was going to be in big trouble when her dad realized that his weed was gone. She became so caught up in the fear of getting in trouble that she made up this big lie and even told a cop that she found it in his apartment and flushed it down the toilet. I was amazed at the extent people would go to in order to protect their lies.

When I walked in the door that night, I got the first and last whooping that Mom ever gave me. She asked me where I was, and I told her. I'm sure she knew I was high at this point. She started swinging the belt at me, and I just stood there, looking at her. When she went to swing it at my arms, I reached out and grabbed the belt. She then grabbed my arm so that she could swing harder.

With each welt of the belt against my skin, she became tired, and I continued to look at her as she began to pant. She was wearing herself out swinging so hard at me. Even though it hurt physically, I was so emotionally and mentally blocked from reality that I didn't even care. I refused to give her the satisfaction of seeing that it hurt. After what seemed like forever being hit with that belt, she finally let go and stopped. She then walked out of the room and never said anything else to me about it.

I pretty much secluded myself from everyone. I stayed in my room, staring at the ceiling or writing poems. I did not talk much to anyone in the house anymore. Allie was now pregnant and had moved out of the house. She had gotten married to a guy she met. She said that he accepted her baby even though he knew that my nephew was not his baby. I was so happy that I was going to have a little nephew. I didn't see much of my sister during this time.

On the day we got the call that she was in labor, I was very excited because my little nephew was soon going to be born. I ducked around the hospital hallways, trying to get a sneak peak of what was going on in the room. I could hear my sister crying and yelling that she couldn't do it. After a short bit, they whisked her away to surgery, and I met my nephew shortly after. As I looked through the glass at him—as he was in the little incubator in the nursery—for the first time, I felt happy about something again. He was a big baby, and he was perfect. He had such long legs and big hands, but he was so precious.

I had no idea that, a couple of years later, I would meet the man who would introduce me to a world of hate and betrayal that was even bigger than what I already had and would make me question myself as a person. Just when you think things cannot get any worse, they do.

Chapter 10

I continued to look for a way out of the life I was living at home. I was at least hanging out with a few of my good friends outside of the house. Holly, Brandy, and Crystal were my best friends at this time. We would hang out and have sleepovers, prank-call people, and go to the movies. When I was with them, things felt normal. Holly and I seemed to be more of the daredevil type because she had started dating African American guys as well, although her parents were not on that either.

But things at home continued to become rough. I continued to deal with physical abuse from Wayne daily. He pushed me into a direction that I didn't want to take. I was looking for any way out, any escape from my every day torture. At the age of fifteen, my best friend, Holly, introduced me to a guy named Ricardo, whom she had met one day while she was in Tasters. He was working at Tasters Restaurant. He was eighteen. She talked about how cute he was and how she had gone out with him one night. I should have known that this was not a good idea considering she had already given him a blowjob. The types of friendship that she and I had were so different. We never kept secrets from each other. She knew how my life at home was, and I knew how hers was. All my friends had already had sex but me. I honestly just was not interested in it. Not only had the only person that I cared about been taken away from me, but the continuation of attempts to being pushed into relationships with other men just because they were white honestly made me not even think about having sex.

The lies began the moment I began talking to Ricardo. He told me that he was a Mexican and that he was in a gang. He said that his mother died from breast cancer. As time passed, his fake stories continued. He called me one day and told me his father was dying and that he had to rush to the hospital to go see him. Later, he said that when he got there, he was just in time to see his father take his last breath. These were only a few of the lies he told me right from the beginning. It was only months later that I found out that the man I was dealing with was a pathological liar who believed his own lies.

Ricardo began to control every decision I made. He would call me throughout the night and made me stay on the phone with him all night, even though he knew that I had to go to school the next morning. He had a way of making me feel guilty if I told him I had to get some sleep. Several times, I would hang up the phone, and he would call back continuously so I would answer to keep from getting in trouble with my mom. At times, I would fall asleep on the phone, and he would cuss me out, telling me how rude I was to him. Ricardo began to come over to the house. When I told them that he was Mexican, my stepdad began to call him a sand nigger and wetback. He would say, "What in the hell is wrong with you?"

After a fight one night at home, I talked to Holly, and she asked me if I wanted to run away. I told her yes. I asked her where we would go, and she said, "I don't know anywhere but here." That sounded so good to me. She told me that she would be by my house that night around 2:30 a.m. She said that she would knock on my window and that she would be parked across the street in the alley. That night, I lay in my bed, nervous but excited. I was scared for her because I knew what her dad would do to her if she got caught. She literally had planned to push their car down the long winding driveway before she started it so that she wouldn't wake them up. I honestly thought that she wouldn't pull it off.

At 2:00 a.m., I sat up in bed and pulled the curtain to the side as I watched out the window for any sign of headlights. There were none. I lay back down and continued to look up at the ceiling. I saw a beam of light that came across the window, and I jumped up. Then I saw a car in the alley, and then the lights flickered off. I knew it was her. My heart racing, I saw her get out and run across the street toward the front of my house. As she ran up to my window, she lightly tapped, and I looked out. She asked me if I was ready to go. Right then, I had this feeling inside me that I couldn't explain. It was that feeling that you feel like something is very wrong or is going to go very wrong. Even though I wanted to leave and never look back I knew that this was not how that was going to happen.

Not now, not like this. So, I told her I can't go girl. I am sorry but I can't. I told her to just go back home and we would need to think this out a little further.

The next morning, I went to school, and she was not there. I was so scared. Where was she? I was called to the office, and they asked me if I knew where she was. I told them no. That afternoon, I got a call from her mom, and she told me that Holly was in a lot of trouble for stealing her car. I played it off and acted like I didn't know. I asked her where she went, and her mom told me that Holly had made it to Memphis. Then she realized she didn't know where she was going from there or how she was going without money. Her mom told me that Holly would be grounded for a long time. I was heartbroken. Why didn't she listen to me? I knew it didn't feel right.

I got a call from Ricardo one afternoon. He said that he needed to come over to tell me something. As he arrived, I noticed that he had shaved his head. He said that he was joining the army and that he was leaving that day for basic training. I knew that something seemed odd about this because he hadn't even graduated from high school nor had he gotten his GED. I was young and just felt like maybe he knew something that I didn't. He went through the motions of asking me if I would wait for him and told me he would call me as soon as he was able to. I told him that with the way things were in my life, I couldn't make him no promises.

Months passed by, and I never heard a word from him. Finally, one day, Mom called me in the living room to tell me that she had spoken to his aunt Jolie in Illinois and that she was informed of the lies he had been telling. She said that his mother and father were very much alive and that he was not in the army. She said that he had gotten kicked out of his grandma's house in Lilbourn for stealing her car and that he had come to stay with her. She said that he was doing the same stuff with her and that he wouldn't be there long either because she was not going to tolerate it.

A few weeks passed, and the phone rang. It was him. I was so furious because of the lies he had told. I literally felt like I did not know who he was at all. He had an excuse for each lie he told. A week or so later, he showed up at my house, saying he was back from basic training. This guy! I tell you—even after calling him out on his lies, he still continued to stick to his story. He slowly began to stop me from talking to any of my friends.

I came home from school one day and called to say he had gotten us a place to stay. He said that his grandparents had rental property and that they were going to let him rent a house for us. My heart was telling me "Don't do it" due to the fear of how he would be if I was alone with him for any given amount of time, but given the circumstances at home, I didn't think things could be much worse. When I told Mom about it, she never asked questions or debated. Instead, she helped pack my things and loaded them into the car and dropped me and my belongings off at the new house.

So, there I was, fifteen and already moving out. I was to figure out this thing called life on my own out there with a man I obviously did not know any truth about. Mom never said anything. She never offered advice or even said it was a bad idea, even though I knew it was. I knew deep down that she was glad I was leaving, as this would put a halt to some of the problems in her household.

Within the first month of moving in together, I found out I was pregnant. I continued to go to school until the morning sickness got so bad that I couldn't go or would miss my ride to school. Ricardo's jealousy and control issues began to worsen as the days went by. He used to suck hickeys on my neck, arms, and chest area just to "claim his territory." I was so embarrassed at school. My coach would call me the hickey queen. I would laugh it off, but deep down, I was embarrassed. Ricardo stopped me from going back to school, threatening me by saying that he would kick me out on the streets if I went. I was an honor roll student and had dreams of going to college, but now my lifelong dream had been eventually crushed. I thought that with me being a good student and never missing school, at least one person in school would be concerned or ask questions. Not one phone call, not one house visit—nothing from any of them. Instead, I was dropped from school due to absenteeism. Homeschooling was not offered to me. So, there I was, a fifteen-year-old high school pregnant dropout. I had no idea what I was going to do.

He began drinking and smoking weed daily. His outrage and jealousy eventually turned worse. I began working as soon as I was of legal age just to make money to support myself. He wouldn't work, and he provided me with nothing, and now I had a baby I would have to support as well. I was unsure how I was going to survive, but I knew that I had to do it on my own. After my son was born, I finally felt like I had a reason to live. He brought life back to me. Holding him, rocking him, and seeing him smile, I felt loved and appreciated. I could look into his eyes as he looked back at me, and somehow, I felt like he knew I needed him as much as he needed me. For once, I knew what it felt like to be truly loved.

The empty lot where the home stood where years of abuse would occur. The house was demolished after my mom sold it to the neighbor years after I moved out.

Chapter 11

Who would have ever thought that the next two years would be so rocky? As Ricardo continued to sleep around, drink, and smoke, I managed to get my GED. I was so happy that I could now do something to help better myself. Ricky had turned two years old, and I decided that I was going to pursue my lifelong dream of becoming a nurse. After two years of being confined to the house with no friends, having a watchdog sit while I was at work to make sure that I didn't talk to anyone, and rarely seeing any of my siblings, my world became very lonely. Every now and then, I would hear from Mom. She would buy something for Ricky, and she would drop it off and leave. Ricardo grandmother and I became very close. She treated me like a daughter. We would sit up late at night and watch Lifetime or sit on her porch and drink tea, just talking about life.

Ricardo was not fond of the idea of me going to college. I knew that I had to do something to better my life and my son's. I was accepted in nursing school and began my first semester. It felt good to be back on track with the goals that I had for myself. One night, I came home from school, and he told me that he was going to Ohio to visit his family and that he was taking our son with him to meet the family. I was reluctant at first because I had only met his family once prior to this.

I decided to let him go against my better judgment since I was in school and would not be able to go with him. After two weeks of being gone, he called me and told me that he wasn't coming back. My son was now almost five hundred miles away from me, and I felt completely useless. He began to tell me that I needed to come up there with them and quit school. He would say that my son needed me and that if I wanted him, I needed to come get him. I was still a young parent with no one I felt I could lean on to help me. I had no faith in the police department from my previous run-ins with them. So, I decided I had to fix this on my own.

I dropped out of nursing school moved to Ohio to get my son. He just didn't realize this was short term for me. It was those first few weeks of being in Ohio around his family that I realized how troubled this man really was. He hadn't had a relationship with his family in years. He had a long history of drinking, stealing, drugs, and gang activity. I found myself being left at home with my son alone while he went out to party. He left me without transportation and no money to buy diapers, milk, or clothes. He left me without any form of communication.

I had begun to walk to the payphone in the afternoon when I knew he would be gone, and I would call Mom collect. I hated to swallow my pride and tell her what was going on, but I needed help from somebody. I was broke, alone, and had no way to get away from this monster. She never really asked too many questions. She did make the comment that she was glad that I finally came to my senses—for whatever that was worth at the time. My hate toward Ricardo grew with each minute that passed. The sexual abuse I got from him took a whole different turn. I would try to keep myself surrounded by other people in his family to prevent some of the torture.

Many nights, I would lie in bed and pretend to be asleep, hoping that he would just lie down and go to sleep. But shortly after, I would feel him start to tug at my clothes. I would tell him to stop and would try to pull away from him, only to have him drag me back and squeeze me so hard I could hardly breathe while he penetrated me from the back. I began to be numb, and the tears eventually stopped coming. I would just lie there and pray that it would soon come to an end. I would lie there in the fetal position, and as he finished and got up, he would say, "You ain't even a good fuck anyway." I would lie there and think back to the feeling I had when I was with Greg. We were not sexually involved, but we were mentally and emotionally connected. I knew in my heart that this was not what a relationship was supposed to be.

Times were growing desperate, and I had to do something. Even though the relationship I had with Mom was not healthy, my heart knew that I could call on her for help. So I had to reach out and put a plan in motion. I continued to call her collect every chance I got so that she could help me put together a plan to get back to Missouri. I told Ricardo that day that my son and I were going to go home for Thanksgiving so that I could spend time with my mom since I had not spent a holiday with her in quite some time. I told him that we would be riding the Greyhound Bus back to Missouri. I had to think of a way to put it nicely for him to let us leave.

His mother became quite upset that we were leaving. I think she knew that once we left, we would not be back. After hours of arguing and fighting over this, his mother decided that if we went, then he had to go too. I was so mad at her. Truth is, I think she knew we were leaving for good and she did not want Ricardo left there. She turned her head the other way and ignored the hell that I was going through while I was there. She didn't want him there either. It wasn't like she really cared anyway. When she was mad at him, she took it out on me. I was the only one of us working. It was freezing cold outside in Ohio in November, and I recall walking an hour to get to work by 7:00 a.m. because no one offered to take me. I recall walking through a snowstorm with almost two feet of snow on the ground for at least three miles to the store to get diapers, and she never offered a ride. I waited in the store long enough to warm up some just to turn around and walk the three miles back.

As I packed our things to go, I knew this was out of spite. She didn't want him to stay there, and she hated me for this. For me, my nightmare would continue. At this point, I didn't care. I just wanted to be back to a place with some sense of security, even if it meant going back to nothing.

After returning to southeast Missouri, I was no longer allowed to be around anyone other than Ricardo and his family. I was beginning to lose my mind. His drinking turned into an everyday event. He started experimenting with pills along with alcohol and weed by this point. The love I had for my son was the only thing that kept me going. But even with my love for him, sometimes at night, I would lie in bed and cry myself to sleep and pray to never wake up again. I had never been so degraded and humiliated in my life. He would forcefully grab my hair and force me to give him oral sex. As he held my head there, I would feel myself start to gag and eventually throw up. As I tried to pull away, he would shove me down and say, "Bitch, you ain't finished. You threw that shit up. Now eat it." My confidence as a human being was stripped away from me, and I no longer wanted to be a part of this world.

The Unforgivable

Chapter 12

With only my money coming in, I barely had enough to pay the bills. Once again, I decided I had to do something to provide for my child and me, so I decided that I would begin nursing school again. On the first day of nursing school, I found out I was pregnant again. This was it. I had to do this. During nursing school, I found a whole different appreciation for living. Even though my life was very dysfunctional, I loved going to school just to talk to others about the normal lives that they were living. I was never really able to elaborate on my home life from pure embarrassment and shame, so the drive in me was stronger now than ever before. I could not give up. I had to do this for us. This was our only chance at freedom.

I had my little girl a few months before graduation. I was so thankful for my OB-GYN, Dr. Poole, who helped me accomplish the goal. I had her on a Friday and returned to school on Monday. I finished nursing school while working a full-time job and taking care of my two babies. The exhaustion from lack of sleep, being overworked, and just pure physical exhaustion was taking a toll on me.

Ricardo's jealousy and anger toward me continued to grow as he did not like me being around other people, but he also knew that he was not able to take care of the children on his own. His day consisted of drinking and getting high. I had to deal with things a woman wouldn't dream of going through with a stranger, much less the man who fathered her children. The hate that I had for him was like a fire burning inside me that I couldn't put out. The only thing that kept me going was my children.

I would periodically go over to Mom's to see my little brothers and talk to her. It was strange how, now that I wasn't living there, we could hold normal conversations and she didn't look at me with such hate.

I was sitting at my mom's house one day when I picked up the newspaper and began to read. My heart sank, and my eyes filled with tears. The only guy in my life who meant anything to me had been arrested and sentenced to prison. I dropped the newspaper and walked to the bathroom to be alone. As I turned on the water faucet to drown out the sound of my sobbing, the uncontrollable tears fell down my face. My heart was broken. Not only did I not have closure with us, but now I felt I would never have the opportunity to tell him how I felt about him then—and even still.

After I graduated from nursing school, I began my career as a nurse. My outlook on life was finally changing. The feeling of going to work, taking care of others, and saving other people's lives was amazing. The only thing was, I could save everyone else but I couldn't save myself. I was a prisoner in my own personal prison—right in my own home.

We were now living in a small house down the road from Mom's. Kaitlynn was now almost eight months old, and Ricky just turned four. We had a little birthday party for him the day before. I was working the night shift at the nursing home and was on, day twenty-two straight. I was exhausted. I came home that morning, fed Kaitlynn, and lay down. I could not even remember falling asleep. I thought I was dreaming that I could smell smoke—only it wasn't a dream.

I rolled over and barely opened my eyes to see the flames lapping under the ceiling and into the living room from the kitchen. The smoke was thick and black. I jumped up and grabbed Kaitlynn out of the baby bed and began yelling for Ricky. Ricardo jumped up from the bed and went looking for him. He found Ricky hiding under the bed in his room. I took him and Kaitlynn and ran down the street to Mom's. I was so out of breath by the time I got there that all I could say was "Fire!" She instantly knew and began calling the fire department.

I was finally getting something positive in my life, but now it was all gone. Everything I owned burned up in that fire that day or was damaged by smoke and water. Now I had to find another place to live. We went to stay at his grandparents' house for a little while until we could find a place. Shortly after, I managed to get an apartment on the same street as the house that burned in New Madrid.

My little girl just turned sixteen months, and once again, he decided we were going back to Ohio. I know you're probably thinking why I didn't leave him, why I didn't tell someone, why I went back. This was an experience that I was living in since I was fifteen years old. He was like the abusive stepfather that I had grown up with. I had no say in anything. I had nowhere to go. He had me knocked down mentally that I thought I had to go. Mom and I were barely speaking. She had only seen the kids maybe once since Kaitlynn was born, and I rarely saw Allie. So once again I was alone. The few things we could pack up, we did, and those we couldn't was left behind in the dumpster.

Chapter 13

We moved back to Ohio, but this time, we were living with his brother and his girlfriend. We all seemed to get along well. After being there a short time, I knew this was not going to work out. Ricardo had always had a jealous issue with his brother, and for some reason or another, he felt like his brother and I were messing around. This created tension in the house. His girlfriend had a different style of raising children, and needless to say, I didn't like the way she was raising her daughter. After being there a month, I was riding around Springfield when I came up on a For Sale sign on a house. It was beautiful and almost sounded too good to be true. But I took a chance, and for once in my life, I won. I bought my first home in 2004. Finally, for once, I was accomplishing some goals. Having a home in my name, where I could protect my children and never have to fear being put out with nowhere to go was the ultimate feeling.

The abuse at home did begin to get worse. A year had passed, and I'd had enough. I began to refuse to have sex with him at all. I began to fight him when he attempted to do so. I would scream or yell. I would sleep with the kids in bed with me just to prevent it. I hated this man. I wanted him nowhere near me. He began to tell me that something was wrong with me. He would call me a fat bitch and call me a lesbian—all in front of the kids on a regular basis. This became the norm for my life. I hated sex. I wanted nothing to do with it. I had begun to question myself and wonder if something was wrong with me.

I made an appointment with my OB-GYN to get a checkup to see if something was wrong with me physically. I explained to her that I was not interested in sex, that it was painful, and that I hated it. I never realized how pathetic that sounded until she looked at me and said, "Crystal, honey, there is nothing wrong with you. Sex is a pleasurable thing—with the right person. Have you ever thought that maybe you are not with the right person?" The light bulb came on. Finally, hearing someone else put it that way helped me realize that you don't have to just stick with something because it's what you are used to. I had to figure something out. Something had to change.

After working all day, I came in one night and got ready to cook my little ones a little supper at around 11:30 p.m. He had been sitting there all-day, playing video games and drinking beer. I barely spoke to him anymore. He did his thing, and I did mine. We were just co-existing at this point. I was so exhausted I didn't even want to eat anything myself. I made the kids a plate and went upstairs to go to bed. As I lay sleeping in bed, I suddenly I felt him on my back. He pushed my head down into the pillow, and he pulled my shorts down. I tried to fight him back, but he pushed my head farther into the pillow.

My screams were muffled by the pillow. He snapped at me, "Be quiet. You're gonna wake the kids up." He thrust inside me, and I instantly felt like throwing up. I tried to squirm out from under him as he continued to hold my face down with his left hand and my arms down with his right hand. Shortly after, he got up and, with a smirk, said, "Why do you have to act like that? You could at least act like you like it." After a year of having no sex with this man, I had begun to thank God for answering my prayers and providing him with someone else to have sex with. He continued his escapades with multiple women here and there. At least I didn't have to worry about it. But once again, I was let down.

I had started talking to Mom more often on the phone now. Our relationship seemed to get better while I was away from there. I had started feeling sick. At this point, I was sick from everything.

One day, I talked to her on the phone, explaining how sick I felt, and she said, "Are you pregnant?"

I said, "I have to have sex to get pregnant, Mom."

She was aware of the problems that we were having, but I kept everyone in the dark about the abuse and torture that I went through daily. I was embarrassed and ashamed to tell anyone. She talked me into getting a pregnancy test. It was positive. As I sat in the bathroom and the tears rolled down my face, I couldn't believe what I was seeing. This could not be true. I never believed in abortion, but my world was too full as it was. I could barely provide for myself and the other two. What was I supposed to do now?

After finding out I was pregnant, I knew that this was it. Something had to be done to end this vicious cycle. I felt that with me being pregnant, then no one else would want me. Months passed and the state of depression, I was in got deeper and deeper. I still was unwilling to accept being pregnant. I kept telling my OB-GYN that there was no way this could be possible, but he confirmed that it was real and that, in nine months, the baby stork would come and there would be a no return-to-sender label. He made me smile as he joked about the situation. If only he knew the real situation . . .

Mom and Bub decided to come up and stay with me at the end of my pregnancy to help out and keep me company. This was a relief. My mom and I had never been able to have that mother–daughter bond, so this was it. We would sit up and work puzzles together. We went shopping and took the kids to the park. One night, as we sat up in the baby room, putting the crib together, I realized how sick she was getting. I could hear her wheezing from across the room. When I asked her if she was okay, she said she was. But I had never heard her like this before. She had a chronic cough from smoking, but this was something new. I told myself that after I had this baby, it would all be over. I couldn't and wouldn't continue to live my life like this.

Chapter 14

After my precious little baby boy Trenton was born, the roller coaster of mental depression soon set in. I was lost in a world of my own regrets and self-pity. I felt so guilty and ashamed that I couldn't even pick him up without the hatred of this man rushing through me. I didn't want this man to have anything to do with something so pure and precious to me. It took weeks for me to get through that frame of mind. I couldn't blame this innocent baby for the way he was brought into this world. I could only love him harder and stronger because of the monster he had as a father.

I had always dreamed of my children living in a perfect world, having a mother and a father and living in a normal family setting. I knew this dream would never come true with this man. My children witnessed the fighting, the drinking, the drugs, and the turmoil that took place daily. This was not the life that I wanted my babies to live. I was so afraid to leave my children with him when I went to work. Many nights, when I came home from work, they hadn't been fed or bathed.

One afternoon, I left for work, and something inside me was telling me something was wrong. I tried to shake the feeling and continue with my routine of taking care of my patients. My inner instinct as a mother and as a woman was always right. I attempted to call him on my break to check on the kids. There was no response. I continued to call multiple times, without any success. So I finally caved and called his mother to go over and check on the kids.

After about thirty minutes, she called me back, and in a frantic voice, she stated, "I am here at the house. Ricky opened the door for me after knocking several times. Ricardo is on the couch, and I can't get him to wake up. I have shaken him and yelled at him, and he will not wake up."

My heart sank, but in a wicked kind of way, I could only pray that he had finally done it, that he had finally overdosed and killed himself. I know that was wrong to think, but anyone who dealt with what I did would understand where I was coming from. The only thing I was worried about was my children. I told her I was on my way.

Upon pulling up in front of the house, I noticed things were completely off. The blinds had been pulled clear up to the top of the tall bay windows. Ricky and Kaitlynn were running around the house. Things were pulled out from everywhere. The house was a disaster. Trenton, four months old, whom I had left sleeping in the pumpkin seat when I left for work at 1:30 p.m., had rolled himself out of the pumpkin seat and was crawling around on the floor, crying at the top of his lungs. By this point, it was 6:30 p.m. The anger inside me kept me from even caring about the monster not responding on the couch.

I picked my baby up out of the floor. He was starving and wet. He had cried for so long his little voice was hoarse. As I held him in my arms and tried to soothe him, I couldn't control the anger anymore. I walked over to the couch, where Ricardo lay barely breathing, and started kicking the couch. I yelled at him a few times, and he finally rolled over and said, "What do you want?" I couldn't say anything. I was at a loss for words. I took my children upstairs and could only hope that he would go to sleep and never wake up. He was pissed that I called for his mom to come over and didn't care that I had to leave work to come check on my babies.

The next couple of months would be my life-changing event. He continued to drink, get high, and sleep around. I got a call from my neighbor while I was at work, and she asked me if my sister was in town. I told her no, and she informed me that Rick had brought another woman in the house who looked sort of like me so she thought it was my sister. Once again, I left work and headed home, hoping this would be the end of it all. As I pulled up in the front of the house, the woman came running out the front door, and he soon followed her. I started yelling, "Who is she?" He continued to get in the car with her, and I told him not to come back.

It wouldn't be long after that that I would find out that she was pregnant. The moment I found out I started crying. I had never been so happy about anything in my life. Finally, this was it for me. My problem that I had dealt with for nine years was now becoming someone else's problem. The next day, he left the house, and as he was leaving, I gathered all his clothes and boxed them up. I had the locks changed and called him and told him his stuff was on the porch and that he had a couple days to get it or it was trash. He came and got his things, and that was the end of that.

Chapter 15

My life was finally starting to look up. I was in strange surroundings. I had been secluded from everyone. I had no family and, of course, made no friends here. I was introduced to a lady who would become my best friend. She began watching the kids for me while I worked. She knew the struggle that I was in and was very helpful to me. I finally began to feel like I had a life.

I never knew what it felt like to not have every minute, choice, thought be controlled by someone; I had been literally programmed. I went to the grocery store and was out within thirty minutes. I looked down as I walked and never looked at someone when they talked to me. I looked in the mirror and saw this horrible person. Self-confidence did not exist in my dictionary. I didn't know what it felt like to be free, but now I was finally free from my own prison. I began enjoying taking my children to the park, only looking over my shoulder to assure myself he wasn't around.

Just when things were starting to look up, my physical condition began to deteriorate. I was sure it was from all the stress and abuse that I had been through. I was so depressed—drowning in bills I couldn't pay, formula I couldn't afford to buy, diapers I couldn't afford to get. I began working as many hours as possible to dig myself out of the grave that he had put me in. I was just thankful that I had not let him put the dirt on top of me yet. I continued to get sicker.

At this time, I found out that I was having major thyroid issues. Flipping from hypo- to hyperthyroid was exhausting. The medicine I had to take made me very sick, yet the doctors were baffled as to what was causing this. I didn't care about living anymore. I continued to work daily, even though I felt like doing nothing. At work, I was going into patients' bathroom to vomit in between med passes just to get me through the shift. I came home one day, and I was in so much pain and was weak and sick that I asked Ricky to call his father to see if he could come get them for a couple of hours so that I could sleep some of it off.

I could hear Ricardo say, "Dad, Mom is sick. Can you come get us for a little bit while she takes a nap?" After hearing his father's response, Ricky looked at me and, with a sad face, said, "Dad said, 'Sounds like a personal problem,' and he can't." From that point forward, my days of asking him to do anything was over. I didn't want him around at all.

After a while, I completed treatment and was on the mend. I had begun taking medication for depression and anxiety and was feeling a little better mentally. I had met a guy at work who was quite a bit older than me. He was Jamaican and ex-military. His personality was wonderful. We began just hanging out and talking. It felt good to have a conversation with another adult again.

He asked me to come over to his house one night. I was scared and reluctant to become involved because of what I had been through. I told him that I couldn't come unless the kids could come too. He took to the kids quickly. He would buy them ice cream, and we would take them to the park. We went to King's Island and the fair together. The kids enjoyed every moment of it. We continued a relationship for five years. I didn't have him around the kids that often because he had his own way of wanting to raise children.

Soon, he began to change like everyone else had. He started coming over only at night after the kids were already in bed, and he would leave before the sun came up. My heart was set for failure, and I just couldn't see anything coming out of this but failure. I cared about him because of the things that he did for me and my children, but my heart told me from the beginning that he wasn't marriage material. I couldn't see myself spending the rest of my life with him. I couldn't see myself being put aside because of his fear of what someone else would say because of the differences in our age or races.

I decided to go back to nursing school and further my career in nursing. For the first time in our relationship, I began to see another side of him that I had never witnessed. He began to tell me that I didn't need to go back, that it would only hinder my ability as a mother and cut me short financially due to not being able to work as much. I began to weigh the options. I couldn't understand why he was telling me this. Why wouldn't he want me to better myself? Then the comments of jealousy started. "You shouldn't wear that. It makes you look fat." He would tell me that people at work were talking about me. To my knowledge, he hadn't lied to me before, so I believed it. My confidence, which had finally started to build up, was slowly being knocked back down again. I stopped having any relationship with people at work simply because, according to him, I couldn't trust any of them.

As time went on, our relationship started to dwindle. He stopped wanting to go do anything together. He then became so wrapped up in what everyone else thought that he slowly pushed me away. After five years of being together, he bought me a ring, and we talked about getting married. He started telling everyone at work that we had gotten married and told me that I needed to tell them that too. But the more I would try to get us to be more like a family, instead of a "just me and him" type of thing, he would just push back and distance himself.

I finally told him if he wasn't willing to commit to that then we needed to just stop what we were doing. Without reluctance, he decided to end it. A military man, accustomed to his own way of living, couldn't fill the void in my life, and I was unwilling to allow myself to settle for anything less. My heart was broken simply because I had dealt with so much heartache already. Five years of no arguments, no fights, a pure platonic relationship, and the hope of something good happening in my life finally came to a sudden end.

I took that blow to the heart as a lesson learned and accepted the fact that I would never find anyone to take the place of my first love. No one could live up to that expectation. No one could give me that feeling that Greg gave me. At this point, I wasn't looking for love. I wasn't looking for marriage. I was just looking for someone to respect me, love me, and be loyal to me the way a man was supposed to.

Chapter 16

I was back on track with just doing me and providing for my children. Living the life of a single mother of three children and it was rough. I found myself working long hours just to hide the pain and fill the void of being appreciated by someone. My patients were everything to me. The way they looked at me and thanked me for taking care of them meant a lot. I was happy about being the one to hold their hand until they took their last breath. Young mothers thanked me for being the one to rock their sick babies to sleep while they cried uncontrollably, not knowing what to do. I loved my job and what it stood for.

I was so confused about how I could take care of others but couldn't seem to handle the storm that was brewing in my mind every day. No matter how hard I tried, I couldn't fight the feeling of loneliness, sadness, and hurt. The medication was only masking the pain and depression that I felt.

One morning, I got off work and picked the kids up from the babysitter and was on the way to drop them off at school when my little girl says, "Mama, what's it mean if you're bleeding from your wrong spot?" My heart sank as I knew there was no reason my six-year-old little girl should be bleeding. I stopped the car in front of the school and asked her what was going on. She then told me that Tommy at the babysitter had hurt her wrong spot. I tried to stay as calm as I could and not make her feel uncomfortable. I told her that I would handle it and that we would go see the doctor.

That day, charges were filed, and my little girl would have to go through the most extensive medical exam that any adult can ever go through, much less a child. I listened as she cried while they examined her. I held her and tried to tell her it was going to be okay, that Mama was there for her. I had tried so hard to protect my babies from this type of shit. But now my little girl had just been put through it, but I wasn't there to protect her. I couldn't catch a break. I felt like I had failed her. As time passed, since Tommy was a minor, he was given a slap on the wrist and spent a year in juvenile detention and not listed as a sex offender, but my little girl would endure a lifetime of pain from this.

I started a new job. It was a new beginning for me and the kids. I continued in nursing school. My friend Missy had just lost her son, and we were there for each other. It was through the friendship that we shared that I was introduced to her other best friend, Deuce. I had seen him before in passing. He was out there in the streets, doing his own thing. He came over to her house one day while I was there. We spoke a couple of words, and I left. A few minutes later, I received a text from him. Missy had given him my number. We texted back and forth for a few days and decided to hang out the coming up weekend.

I spent the whole week working at the hospital in Columbus. He would text me off and on throughout the day, telling me how beautiful I was and how he couldn't wait for the weekend. He came on very strong—something I was not used to. That Friday, I headed over to Missy's so we could all go out to the movies. Once I got there, he came out to the car and said that Missy was sick and was not going, that it was just going to be the two of us. I started to feel a little nervous because I didn't even really know him.

That night, we decided to just go to the house and watch movies. He had bought a bottle of vodka. We spent the weekend together and got along very well. The kids met him, and he was good around them. They ran and played throughout the house, in the yard, at the park. He bought them candy. He was the first man besides my ex that had ever paid attention to my children. I couldn't help but wonder if it would end like the previous relationship did. We began to spend more and more time together.

I was in class one day when I got a call from Mom, and she told me that my dad had passed away. I was hurt by it because I felt like it was a relationship that I just didn't have. He had begun to call me in the last several months, and we would talk about everything. He would be confused as to whom he was talking to from time to time. Sometimes he would think he was talking to my sister Cheryl. Other times, he would forget how old I was and ask me if I had learned to ride a bike yet and if I could read or write. I was confused, angered, and just annoyed by it, really. I kept thinking in my head that he never wanted anything to do with us. Why didn't he take us that day at the courthouse? I had to push aside those emotions, and for the first time in years, I decided that I was going to make that drive to Tennessee and be there for my oldest brother, Rocky. He deserved that much, and I needed that closure in my life.

That day, I walked into the funeral home and saw my dad lying in that casket. I didn't feel like I was looking at the same man. He had lost so much weight. My brother told me he had been sick and that the medication he had been on had him talking out of his head. Allie and I spent the afternoon with my brother at the funeral, and he took us for a drive around to show us places that we had lived in back then. My memory was blank. Nothing looked familiar to me.

That night, when I got back my house, I realized that my front door had been kicked in. Some things had been stolen from my house. I began to question myself. I called Missy and told her about it. She told me that Deuce did it. I called him, and of course, he denied it. Even though I knew the type of life he lived and the type of people that he hung out with, I believed him.

Over the next several months, I noticed that money from my safe was being stolen, and of course, when asked, Deuce denied that too. I began to see a change in him. He became very agitated and upset when I would not give in to him and give him money or buy him things. He would say, "I will just get it from somewhere else." The more I told him no, the more upset he would get. Once again, I was being shut off from the outside world. My best friend, Susie, was dating his cousin, and she was the only one that I could talk to. She, too, was dealing with the same thing.

I would try to make Deuce leave, but he just would not go. Many times, he would cry and beg me to not leave him, and he would tell me how sorry he was, that he would never do it again. Then he would turn around in a few hours and take a little bit more than he did previously. As the months passed, I could only hope that things would get better. I was only setting myself up for the biggest heartbreak and emotional roller coaster I had ever imagined.

I became very close with his family. His mother was like a mom to me. We talked about everything. There wasn't anything we did not talk about. I only hoped that one day he would see that I cared and that things would change. That hope only led him to be that much more hateful and demeaning to me. I tried to preoccupy myself with work and the kids to help take away the hurt I was feeling inside. Even though I talked to his mom, I couldn't tell her everything that was going on. I couldn't let her know that her one and only son, whom she loved so much, was really a monster.

It was a Friday night. The kids were gone for the weekend, so Deuce decided that we would go out, get a few drinks, and chill. As we headed over to his friend's house, he took a couple of ecstasy pills out of his pocket and said, "Here—one for you and one for me." I figured we wouldn't be over here long given the fact that once you take one, you must be on the move and drinking before they kick in. We took it and went into his friend's house.

I already felt awkward since he hadn't ever really had me around his friends. So I took a seat on the couch in the front room. As they sat and smoked, I could feel the ecstasy start to kick in. I began to sweat. I waited . . . and waited . . . Finally, after what seemed forever—and a few blunts later—he was ready to go. As we walked to the car, he takes another ecstasy pill out of his pocket and says, "Here, let's halve it." At this point, I wasn't really feeling nothing from the first one being I was just sitting for hours after the first one. I already knew this was going to be a long night, and I knew better than to say no. So I took the second half.

As we are driving, he had me pull over to another guy's house so that he could run in quick. I pulled up to the drive, and he jumped out of the car. As I sat there, I looked down and realized he had left his phone lying on the seat. He was just on it, so the screen was unlocked. I didn't know if it was my heart or the effects of the ecstasy pill telling me to look at it, but I picked it up and started scrolling through the phone.

I knew he wouldn't be in there long, especially when he realized he didn't have his phone. To no surprise, it didn't take long. Immediately, I saw the text messages from other females—several of them—whom he had been texting and receiving sexual photos from. My heart began to race. The passenger door opened, and he got in. He snatched the phone out of my hand.

I yelled at him, "What in the hell are you doing? Who are they?"

He immediately became defensive. "It's just bullshit. They don't matter." The more he lied to me, the madder I got. I started yelling, "Get out of my fucking car!"

He refused to get out. At this point, I was so amped from effects of the pill that I punched the gas, swerving and flying down the street. I just wanted to go home. I wanted to be as far away from him as possible. I figured once I went home, he would leave. That always seemed to work. If I was mad, he would just leave and then show up again hours later.

He started yelling, "Slow this damn car down!"

I was so hurt and felt so betrayed that I didn't care what happened at this point. We finally made it back to the house. As I walked into the back door and headed toward the living room, I felt my neck snap back. It took all about three seconds for me to realize that he had just snatched me by my hair. As I practically fell back onto him, he grabbed me by my throat. As I started to fight against him, the pressure of his squeeze on my throat tightened. As I looked into his eyes while he choked the life from me, I saw a side of him I had never seen.

Without any hesitation, he said in a calm but firm voice, "Don't ever try that shit again. You will never leave me. If anybody leaves, it will be me, and that will be when I am ready."

I could feel my racing heart start to slow down as I choked for air. He released his grip from my throat. My whole body was numb from panic, hurt, betrayal, anger, and pure exhaustion as I fell to the floor. I felt the hot acid rising in my stomach as I began throwing up violently. He walked off and sat down on the couch and fired up another blunt.

As my eyes closed, I wasn't sure if I would wake up in the morning. I prayed that God would never make me go through this again. I prayed that he would end my pain. I began to panic, and my heart started racing. The pressure on my chest felt as if I was going to have a heart attack. I begged

Deuce to call the ambulance. He refused to do it. Instead, he called my friend Susie and told her what I was doing. She somehow got him to call the ambulance. I was relieved as I hoped this would get rid of him. No. Instead he ran around the house, paranoid. He was opening the vents and freaking out, thinking he was going to get arrested.

When the paramedics arrived, they hooked the EKG machine up, and I could see that I clearly was not having a heart attack but that my heart rate was definitely too high. I told the paramedic that I was having an anxiety attack. He asked me if I had smoked marijuana, and I told him no. Deuce then spoke up and said that he had just smoked. After clearing me, the paramedic told me to relax for the rest of the night, and then they left.

Off and on throughout the night, my eyes slightly opened as I lay in my own vomit on the floor. I couldn't find the energy to get up. The room was dark, and there was only the glow of the hallway light in the distance. Then it was quiet, and my eyes closed again.

Chapter 17

My faith was really in question. I just could not understand why I had to deal with the things that I was dealing with. Things would get good for a little bit, then only turn for the worse afterward. The arguments, lying, cheating, stealing, and abuse continued. The hard part about the whole situation was the fact that my children found in Deuce the father that was never there for them. He was good with the kids. They looked up to him. There was a part of me that knew that I was accepting his behavior because I wanted my children to have that relationship that their father was not giving them. I watched my babies sit and wait at the door for their dad while at the babysitters on his weekend to pick them up. He never showed up. They would have the sitter call his phone multiple times, only for him not to answer. Seeing the sad, puffy faces of crying themselves to sleep after waiting for him hurt me to the core and made me hate him even more.

Deuce did at least respect the kids enough and not show his fits of anger and aggression around them. That was the hard part. On the days when I couldn't stand to look at him, I had to pretend that I was happy and that everything was okay. I didn't want my children to see that I was hurt or upset. I especially didn't want them to know what Deuce was doing to me.

He began to steal my car at night, leaving me home with no way to go anywhere. This occurred almost every night. I hid my keys from him at night, and he would look for them. I told him he wasn't going to get them. I could see the anger in his face, but I knew he wouldn't do anything with the kids there. I could only hope that he would call one of his boys to come pick him up.

After a few minutes, he said, "Can you run me across town then since I can't take the car?"

I breathed a sigh of relief. He finally asked me to do something reasonable.

He told the kids, "Your mom will be right back. She's going to run me across town real quick."

As we got into the car, he turned on the stereo. We headed down a dark one-way street. As he started rapping along with the song, and I began to think I should have hidden the keys a long time ago if it was going to be this easy. Before I could get that thought completely through my mind, he grabbed my thigh and punches my leg onto the gas pedal. The car instantly sped up. There were no words from his mouth and no expression on his face. He just stared a head.

I yelled at him to stop, but he continued to punch my foot to the gas pedal. At this point, tears started to fall down my face. I was sure that I was going to hit someone. So to keep from killing someone else, I took the steering wheel and slammed it to the right. Just about ten feet in front of us was a utility pole.

With tears streaming down my face, I said to him, "Let's do this. I'm ready to die if you are." He grabbed the emergency brake, and the car came to a halt as the back end fishtailed in the street.

He said, "You crazy bitch! Take me to my boy's crib."

I began to pull the car into reverse, and at that moment, I felt his grip on the back of my head. He forced my face toward the steering wheel, and blood began to pour from my nose and mouth. He loosened his grip on my hair. I sat there in silence as tears streamed from eyes.

He said calmly, "Don't ever hide shit from me again."

I slowly pulled the car back out into the street. My eyes, nose, and mouth were swollen. I could hardly see to drive. Fighting back the tears, I drove. I couldn't get there soon enough.

Back home, I pulled into the driveway and quietly went through the back door, trying not to wake the kids. Quietly walking down the hallway,

I saw them asleep in their beds. I pulled their doors shut as I walked into the bathroom.

As I stood there and stared at my reflection in the mirror, I couldn't stop the tears from streaming down my face. The blood mixing with the tears ran down my cheeks. I ran the warm water across my face to hopefully wipe away the pain that I had just been through. My face was swollen, my heart was broken, and my spirit was literally ripped from my body. I walked down the hallway into my bedroom, shut the door, and crawled into bed. As I lay there in a fetal position, I thanked God for allowing me to make it back home to my babies.

As I cried, I drifted off to sleep. I was awakened by the sound of the bedroom door opening. I lay there in complete silence, not moving. I knew it was Deuce. I felt him fall onto the bed. He began to pull the blanket off me. He began pulling me closer to him.

I could smell the aroma of alcohol from his breath as he whispered, "Get over here."

I quietly said, "Don't touch me. I hate you for what you have put me through. I hate the person that you are." I never turned to look at him. I just stared at the wall in front of me. He moved away from me. I heard him reach into the nightstand. Then I heard the chamber of the 9 mm pistol click. I continued to lay there in silence.

He stated, "Oh, you hate me, do you? Well, guess what. I hate your white ass too. I will never be with another white bitch. You ain't shit. I got what I wanted. I will just move on to the next bitch, and she won't be white either."

I knew he was saying things that he thought would make me mad. So I continued to lie there and did not respond to him. As I lay there in silence, he continued to rant about how much he hated me. It was at that moment that I felt the coldness of the barrel touch the back of my head, and the click as he cocked the gun. I never moved.

He leaned over and whispered in my ear, "I will blow your brains out."

At this point, I was so furious about what had taken place earlier that I said, "What? You going to kill me with my kids in the next room?"

He stated, "Yeah, they will be fine. You got family to take care of them."

I closed my eyes and prayed to go to sleep and never wake up. He grabbed my arm and pulled me over onto my back. I tried to pull away from him, but he sat on top of me and held my arms down. I tried to yell, and he took his hand and forced it down, covering my mouth. He told me to shut up. I dug my nails into his arms as he held me down. I tried to kick him, but with the weight of his body on top of me, I realized it was useless.

He started pulling my clothes off. "I'm going to rape you like your baby daddy used to."

I felt my body go completely limp. Those words sent a pain through me that was unexplainable. I never dreamed I would hear him say something so horrific. I could take the beatings a lot better than that. As he thrust into me, I turned to look away from him as the tears ran down my face. He looks down at me and grabs my face to make me look at him. There were no words that I could say to express the humiliation that I felt at that moment. As he gripped my chin in his hand, I spat in his face. He then leaned down toward me and started quenching his mouth to spit. He then began to slowly let the saliva run from his mouth into my nose and eyes. I began to choke as I tried to breathe while his saliva ran up my nose. I was drowning on his spit. I finally stopped fighting him, and he finished.

I slowly turned over and pulled myself as close to the edge of the bed as possible. I lay there in the dark, crying softly and wishing that someday, somehow I would be away from all of this. Then I felt him reach over me and grab the skin on my stomach and clench it, pulling it with force. Then he laughed. He knew that my stomach was my insecurity, and tonight he was pulling all strings to show me how real his hate was for me.

It was in times like these that I would close my eyes and remember the times I was with Greg, remembering the way he used to make me feel. It always helped me get through these moments because I knew that this wasn't the way it was supposed to be. Even though Greg wasn't here, he was still in my heart. He was the reason I was able to keep looking ahead for bigger and better things when it came to relationships. Greg continued to give me hope to not give up on living. That gave me the motivation to keep being the best mother I could be for my children. I knew because I had once felt the feeling of real true love, and I wanted that back. I wanted that for my babies. I wanted them to feel loved, and I wanted them to see me truly happy and loved. I had to keep fighting for what I wanted for me but mostly for them.

Chapter 18

I was sitting in the closet one day, going through pictures and organizing things, when the phone rang. I looked down to see that it was the doctor's office calling me. As I listened to my doctor tell me that my Pap test showed that I had cancer cells and needed surgery, I fell quiet. I called my mom to tell her the news, and I told her that I wasn't sure I could go through this again. She then told me that giving up was not an option, that the kids needed me. Soon after, I graduated from RN school and decided I'd had enough. I was moving back to Missouri.

Deuce told me that he was going to. I tried to dissuade him into not coming by telling him that he would hate it because his family wasn't there. I explained how I had felt the years that I had been in Ohio without my family. I spent the next few weeks packing and was ready for the change. I didn't care if he was coming. One thing that I knew for sure was that if he did, he wouldn't get away with treating me the way he did here. So I was okay with it. I felt that he wouldn't be there long until he would miss his family and kicking it with his boys every night and that he would eventually want to go back.

A week before the move, Deuce decided he wasn't going to Missouri. I was excited. I had talked to Mom, and we arranged everything so I could get a U-Haul. Everything was already planned. On the night before I was scheduled to move, Deuce showed up at the house and said that he was coming as well, so things went a little differently. We made the move to Missouri, and being around my family felt relieving. I never told Mom that Deuce was coming with me. I never talked to her about him and our relationship. I didn't think that she was happy about it, especially when she realized he was black the first day she met him.

The hurt and pain that I had gone through these past three years alone were finally behind me. As the days passed, I begin to see a different side of Deuce. He began to show a caring and loving side that I had not seen before. I was confused. Even though he was finally being nice to me, I still could not get past the hurt he had caused me. After a few weeks, Deuce began to hibernate in the bedroom. He would only come out to eat or go riding with my brother. His jealousy grew stronger. I couldn't leave the house to go anywhere but to work and to Mom's.

As the days passed, I was getting sicker. The cancer was taking a toll on my body. I finally went back to the doctor, and he informed me that I needed to have surgery, which I already knew. He told me that if I wanted children even though my tubes were tied, I needed to reconsider that now because after this surgery, there would be no option for it. At this point in my life, I had three beautiful children and wasn't at a place in my life where I wanted anymore. I especially didn't want any kids with Deuce. I wanted to know his reaction, so that day, when he came home, I told him I needed to talk to him. We sat down at the kitchen table, and I told him what the doctor said. I asked him if he wanted more children, and he said no.

My mind was already made up, but I just wanted to see where his head was. As the night passed, I knew he was in a place in his mind that I didn't dare go. So I left the conversation as it was and left him alone. I was hurt because he never made any effort to comfort me or ask me if I was okay. He didn't ask any questions or offer any support. I don't know why this came as a surprise to me given what I had already been through with him. I guess I was grasping at thin hope of something different.

Within a month of us being back in Missouri, Deuce dropped the bombshell that he had a son. I had no idea. He tried to tell me that he just found out about it, and I would later find out that he knew about it before we moved to Missouri.

I was scheduled to have a hysterectomy to have the cancer cells removed. The days began to get worse. He began to accuse me of cheating on him. He began to slip back into his old ways of stealing the car, my credit cards, and money. I knew in my heart what was about to take place. I just didn't have the strength to fight nor the heart to tell my family of the hurt I was going through. Maybe it was out of fear of being told it was my fault or out of humiliation. Whatever the reason, I stayed to myself and let it all start again.

Many nights, I was awakened to Deuce talking on the phone to other females or waking up to an empty bed as he would slip out after I fell asleep. I had to hide the car keys and my bank cards under Kaitlynn's pillow at night or in her shoes to keep him from taking them. The arguments started, and at this point, I didn't care who knew about it. I had finally reached a point where I didn't care. I was in my familiar surroundings, and I knew at least here he wouldn't kill me and get away with it. So I stood my ground. I wanted him to leave so bad, but he just wouldn't give in.

The hate in me grew stronger. I began to talk to some of my old guy friends about the situation, and a few of them were more than willing of giving Deuce a good Southern beatdown. Then I had to take a step back and question myself. This man was driving me crazy. He was taking me to a place mentally that I didn't want to be. I was stooping to his level.

December 08, 2012

Dear whoever is listening:

I went with my sister today to find an outfit for the work appreciation dinner tonight. I had so much on my mind that I didn't want to be there. I just feel like going to sleep and never waking up. I know that sounds selfish, and maybe it is. But I feel like no matter what I do for him, it's never enough. I have faced the fact that he does not love me the way I want to be loved. I guess I can't fault him for that. I am so mentally broken. I feel like screaming, but there is no one to hear me. I feel like I am trapped inside a box with the same four walls caving in around me every day. My heart can't possibly hurt any more than it already is. I've been disrespected, lied to, and betrayed. Now all I can do is think about what he will do to me next. I know in my heart I can't let this keep happening.

I was on my way home from work, and my best friend, Brandy, called me. She told me that Deuce had started texting her. She said the conversation started out mutual and then he began to pursue her. He was trying to get her to let him come over to her house. He went so far as to tell her when I worked, what time the kids got on the bus—my whole routine. The only thing about it was that he didn't realize that her loyalty to me as a friend was far stronger than his ever was for me. I was dumbfounded about the whole situation, and she forwarded me all the messages from that day.

I walked through the door and saw Deuce in the room as usual. As soon as I walked into the room, he jumped up from the bed and asked how my day was. That was his normal routine when he was texting or talking to someone he shouldn't have been. I snatched the phone from his hand and asked him whom he was talking to. He quickly said, "Nobody." He tried to snatch the phone from my hand, and I threw the phone against the wall. I could see the anger building in his face, but I was so mad and hurt that I didn't care what the consequences might be. I wasn't giving up anymore. I was done.

As I began yelling at him and telling him what I knew about him texting Brandy, he tried to deny it. This just made me madder. I continued to yell at him, calling him a liar and a cheater. He tried to push me out of the bedroom, away from him, but I kept coming back at him. He grabbed me by my arms and shoved me out of the room.

Kaitlynn was in her doorway and began to cry. "Mom, please don't."

I told her to go into her room and stay there. Then I went right back at him. He raised his hand up at me, and the look in his face was the same as before. I raised my hand up to push him away, and he grabbed both of my arms, lifted me off the floor, and tossed me down the hallway like a ragdoll. My daughter in her doorway was crying because she had never witnessed this before. I jumped up from the floor and headed back toward the bedroom, and he slammed the door in my face and locked it. I took the kids and went to my mom's just to let the situation settle down.

Mom could always tell when something was wrong. The depression and anxiety attacks were becoming worse. I could hardly talk to her anymore without crying, but I continued to say I didn't know what was wrong with me and blamed it on my long history of depression and anxiety. I've been through years of taking antidepressants and anti-anxiety medication, and nothing was working. I began to question myself as a mother and as a person. How could I let my children live in such an environment where there was no happiness? After a few hours passed, we went back home. As I lay in the bathtub that night, listening to the hum of the TV in the next room, I began to replay all the events that had taken place in my life. I felt as if I had literally no one to talk to or trust.

Standing and looking at myself in the mirror, I saw a woman who was completely empty inside. Without emotion or fear of anything, I reached into the cabinet and pulled out the box cutter. As I flicked the blade out and looked down at the shiny metal, I held it close to my arm. As I pushed the tip into my skin, finally, I felt something—the feeling of pain but exhilaration as I slid the blade down my arm while the blood poured from my arm. Finally, a feeling came over me, something that I could control, but adrenaline released from my body and gave me a feeling of strength, a feeling that I could not explain. Finally, I felt relief from all the hurt that I had gone through and continued to go through.

Chapter 19

The days were winding down to my surgery day. Deuce and I were barely speaking to each other. He kept telling me that he was leaving and going back to Ohio, and I could only hope that was the case. His excuse was that he wasn't going to leave until I had my surgery and knew that I was okay. I knew it was an excuse because he had yet to ask me how I felt or comfort me in any way.

To whoever is listening:

After this surgery, I'm unable to work and have no money to pay the bills. I try to pull things together to survive. He couldn't care less. Tonight, he comes out of the room and slaps at me and pushes his hand into my face. The paycheck he receives, he spends on lottery and weed. He tells me he doesn't care whether I have money or not to pay the bills or buy groceries. He goes and buys himself pizza and eats in front of us like we are nobody. Then he tells me he doesn't give a damn about the kids. He steals my debit card and takes the little amount of assistance I'm able to get while I'm not working. So there goes the rent money, and hell, it isn't even enough. I have become numb to everything.

Finally, when I was able to get back to work, I continued to work daily through the pain of it all. My routine was the same. After work, I came home to an unclean house, the kids needing to be fed and asking for help with their homework, and the laundry to do. All the while, Deuce lay in the bedroom all day or ran the streets.

One rainy day, I left work to come home for my lunch break. I went into the house and made myself a bowl of soup. As I sat at the kitchen table in silence, I heard Deuce come out from the room. He sat down at the table and asked how work was going. He started a conversation, which I knew would never turn out good.

I kept it simple and replied, "Fine."

He then proceeded to ask me if he could drop me back off at work and use the car. I quickly finished my lunch as I knew this conversation was leading to a fight.

As I put my dish into the sink, gathered my things, and walked toward the door, I replied, "No, you can't." I instantly saw the anger in his face.

He stepped toward me and replied, "Yes, I am."

I backed away from him and stepped toward the table. I told him, "I have to get back to work. I can't do this right now."

Deuce picked up the broom from beside the refrigerator, and before I could flinch, he snapped the broom handle down on my hand that rested on the back of the chair. Instantly the swelling and bruising began, and the deformity of my pinky finger was evident. He walked back toward the kitchen, and I turned and ran out of the door toward the car. The pain throbbing in my hand, I fought to get the car door open as fast as I could. I locked the doors quickly behind me and started the car. He came running out the back door behind me as I pulled from the driveway.

Tears of anger and pain streamed down my face as I now had to think of an excuse to tell my workplace as to why I couldn't go back to work. I thought of a quick lie to get past the humiliation of the incident and told them I had smashed my finger in the car door and had to go to the ER. He began texting and calling me, and I refused to answer. Three hours later, I was on my way back home with a broken finger. I scrolled through the multiple hate-filled text messages he sent while I was gone.

This was always what happened. Many times, Deuce would tell me how much he hated me and how I deserved everything I got. He would say he was going to kill me when I came back home. Then he would flip the script and tell me how sorry he was, that he didn't mean to do it, and that he just didn't know what came over him. He would tell me how much he loved me and didn't want me to leave him. Of course, if I didn't respond, he would flip back to hating me and wishing I was dead. I had become so immune to his words and crazy behavior. His words no longer hurt my feelings because I no longer had feelings to hurt. Hell, if this is what love was supposed to feel like or be like, I could do without it.

To whoever is listening:

The medicine I take seems to be working to some degree, or maybe it's just making me not give a shit. The things that used to bother me, I don't even care about them anymore. He constantly picks fights with me. Most of the time, we don't even sleep in the same room anymore. The kids have begun to feel like he doesn't want to be around them. As soon as they come home, he goes into the bedroom and doesn't even talk to them. He gets mad and makes fun of the way he broke my finger before. That kind of behavior proves to me that he never gave a damn about me. My kids are suffering from my stupidity. I can't afford to keep my head above water. I can't be the mother I want to be to my children, and they are suffering because of me. Once again, he busts my nose tonight. He starts mocking me, stating, "Go cut yourself, but make sure you do it the right way." I've never thought someone can break me down the way that he has. He looks me in the eyes and tells me that he hates me and that he's going to kill me.

After my surgery, I was on the road to recovery. Deuce continued to tell me that he was going back home. He continued to cheat, steal, and lie. I figured we would all be better off if he did go back home. One day, I was at work, and a feeling came over me that just didn't seem right. My brother Tony and his girlfriend, Chelsea, had stayed the night at the house the night before, and they were supposed to leave that morning when Tony had to go to work. I decided to leave work early and go home because something just felt off.

As I walked through the back door, I saw him jump up from the couch—with my brother's girlfriend, Chelsea, beside him—and yank his pants up. The look on his face was priceless. The kids were in my room with the door shut, although they were never allowed there since that was where I kept my gun. She never said a word. He started walking toward me, and at that moment, something came over me. I just snapped.

I asked him, "What in the hell were you doing?"

He said, "Nothing."

I was no fool, nor was I going to be played for one in my own house. I walked past him toward the bedroom. Before he could say anything, I said, "I should blow your fucking brains out, you dirty bastard! How could you? In my own house! With my own brother's girlfriend, who is supposed to be my friend, and my kids in the next room!"

After a couple of seconds, I heard my daughters giggle in the next room, and reality set in. I told him to pack his stuff, that it was over. Even after telling my brother Tony what had happened, he decided to believe Chelsea and Deuce, who both said that nothing happened. So I told him that she was no longer allowed in my house, and he told me if she wasn't allowed there, then he guessed he wouldn't come either. I said, "Fine. That's just how it will be." I had to work another day that week, but I firmly told Deuce that he was leaving that week.

A couple of nights after that, my daughter came to me, and she was crying. I asked her what was wrong, and she told me, "It happened again." I asked her what happened, and she told me that someone had touched her in the wrong spot. My heart dropped because she had been having nightmares since she was sexually assaulted by a Tommy at the babysitter's house in Ohio. She told me that her uncle Tony had come into her room and touched her. Because of the history and trauma, I asked her if she was sure that it wasn't just a dream. She sat there for a minute, and then she said, "Well, maybe it was just a dream." I hugged her and told her that I was there for her and that she could come to me anytime. I told her that uncle Tony would not be staying at the house anymore since she was having those nightmares.

She had no idea what had transpired with Deuce and Chelsea. When Deuce came home from riding with Tony that night, I told him what she said, and Deuce began to call him. He did not answer, and he left a message on his voicemail in a threatening manner. The next morning, Tony called me, and he was crying. He told me he didn't understand why my daughter would say that about him, that he would never do anything to hurt her. I told him that I did not want him coming to the house anymore, that I had to protect her, and that I could not have her feeling threatened in her own home.

I immediately got her back to counseling again. But she would not talk to them, and she hated going. She would go and look at the wall. If they asked her any questions about it, she would get resistant and not answer them. We finally stopped going. But no one did anything any further than that. There was no questioning and no discussions. I was left on my own with this to deal with.

Chapter 20

To whoever is listening:

I knew the time would come that we would have to go our separate ways. I would have to stand up and make a decision that could change my life for better or worse. I am willing to take this chance now. I can't take it anymore. I am tired of hiding the bruises on my body and the hurt in my heart.

We loaded his belongings into my car, and I set out to get rid of the baggage that I had carried for so long. I was no longer afraid for my life. I was finally taking my life back. The drive was the longest seven hours ever. Not one word was spoken. I was exhausted. I pulled into his mother's driveway, and he unloaded his things. He walked to the car door and asked me to come in to rest for a few hours before heading back out on the road. Honestly, I wanted to be as far away from him as possible. I hated the man that he had become, and I knew that if I didn't leave right then, I might not make it out of Springfield alive. Through it all, I knew no one could live up to my expectations. This wasn't what I wanted. The only one person that I wanted was gone.

It was at that moment that I realized I was finally free. As I turned onto the interstate, headed back home, the tears started flowing down my face. I was confused. I didn't know if it was from happiness, betrayal, loneliness, or pure pity.

The depression really sank in when I had to explain to the kids that he wasn't coming back. I took all the blame and told them it was my fault and that I made him go. I told them that he missed his son and family. They were mad and hurt because the man that they knew as their dad was now gone. He didn't respond to any text messages or phone calls that the kids made. This was heartbreaking to me. I never expected him to completely turn his back on the kids like that, and I never expected him to do it the way he did either. My kids were so heartbroken. I was sad to know that my kids were having to deal with this again. I felt sorry for them, but deep down, I also prayed that he would continue to ignore them because I didn't want to have to deal with him in any way possible.

After a few weeks, he had moved on with someone else, and I could finally breathe. The taunts would continue, as he would periodically send me text messages with his new girlfriend wearing the ring that his granny had told him to give to me. That was painful as I was there the day his granny passed away. She would always hold my hand and tell me that God had sent me to her grandson to help him get on the right path. She told me to be patient with him and to stay strong and that things would get better. At times, I felt like I let her down, but in the end, it was him that let her down. She told him when she gave that ring to him that no other woman was to have that ring but me. But he willingly gave them to someone he only knew for a couple of months. His granny knew that I tried my best with him, but I couldn't do it any longer. I would like to say that she was the one who made a way for me to leave him.

Chapter 21

There are things in life that you encounter every minute of each day. Even without knowing the outcome, you have to make decisions about each situation. Some decisions are hasty and irresponsible, and others are simply out of your control. A very special person in my life said something to me that gave me have a whole new outlook on the things that I encountered in my life. Women sometimes accept things as they are and do not look for the greater good. When dogs are kept inside a shock fence, they learn to stay inside the fence because they do not like to be shocked. The shock of the fence hurts; therefore, they develop a fear of the fence and, over time, accept what is inside the fence because that is what they know as their security. They become used to the surroundings and accept them as they are. They watch and see the greater good on the other side of the fence and deep inside they want that new life, but the fear of getting shocked causes them to lose that chance of freedom. There are a few who will eventually jump over the fence and risk the chance of getting shocked so that they can be free from the fear that they have lived in for so long. Sometimes we do things or allow things for all the wrong reasons or for the pleasure of others. But what about me? When would I finally do something for me?

My new journey was finally beginning. I was free. Though I was spiritually, physically, and mentally broken, I was finally free. I was one of those rare few who decided to finally jump over the shock fence to the freedom that was waiting on the other side. The hard part was over. Now I had to pull myself together and get back on track. The days were hard. A part of me was saddened by the fact that my children had lost all respect for men in their lives because the only two men who were there were now gone. They were young and did not understand what was going on. The way they saw it, it was my fault because I was the one who sent them away. I made the choice to take all the blame because I couldn't possibly let them see the pain and hurt that I had gone through just trying to make them happy. It was my job as a mother to protect them from harm at all costs even if it meant taking the blame for something I had no control over.

I began to think and wonder about Greg more than I ever had before. There wasn't a day that went by that I didn't think of him. I wondered how he was doing, where he was, and how his life had turned out. I didn't know if he was married, had children, or where he was. For all these years, this was a chapter in my life that stayed open. I needed some answers, some explanation, some closure. Throughout my life, I expected the men in my life to be like him, to treat me the way he did, to give me the feeling of never wanting to be away from them the way he did. The way we were torn away from each other was something that I never got over.

I began to question if that was the reason my relationships didn't work. So I set out to find answers. I began to search for him harder than I ever had before. I would see pictures of people with the name Greg Thomas, and my heart would drop. But once I saw them up close, I was only heartbroken to see it wasn't him. More than anything, I wanted him to know that, throughout my life, it was him who kept me pushing forward and kept me from giving up because I held on to the feeling that I had when I was with him and continued searching for that feeling. I needed him to know how much he meant to me, even if he had moved on in life.

To be continued . . .

CPSIA information can be obtained
at www.ICGtesting.com
Printed in the USA
JSHW032149201222
35243JS00003B/65